#	Name	Address
37	**Meudon**	13 Onslow Ave,
38	**Selsdon**	16 Macleay St,
39	**Macleay Regis**	12 Macle
40	**Four Macleay St**	4 Mac
41	**Bellevue Gardens**	20 W
42	**Wyldefel Gardens**	8 Wylde St, PP
43	**17 Wylde St**	17 Wylde St, PP
44	**Belvedere**	21 St Neot Ave, PP
45	**19 St Neot**	19 St Neot Ave, PP
46	**Trent Bridge**	17 St Neot Ave PP
47	**The Lachlan**	9-11 St Neot Ave PP
48	**Park View**	7 St Neot Ave, PP
49	**Manchester**	2 McDonald St, PP
50	**4 MacDonald St**	4 MacDonald St, PP
51	**Esquire**	10 Challis Ave PP
52	**10a Challis Ave**	10A Challis Ave, PP
53	**The Clift**	10B Challis Ave, PP
54	**Gloucester Hall**	10c Challis Ave, PP
55	**Twenty**	20 Macleay St, PP
56	**Werrington**	85 Macleay St, PP
57	**Wychbury**	5 Manning Rd, PP
58	**Devere Hotel**	44 Macleay St, PP
59	**Carlysle**	2 Crick Ave, PP
60	**West End**	3 Crick Ave, PP
61	**Byron Hall**	97-99 Macleay St, PP
62	**Tara**	3 Greenknowe Ave, EB
63	**7 Greenknowe Ave**	7 Greenknowe Ave, EB
64	**25 Hughes St**	25 Hughes St, PP
65	**Kanimbla Hall**	19 Tusculum Ave, PP
66	**Gowrie Gate**	115 Macleay St, PP
67	**Metro Theatre**	30 Orwell St, PP
68	**Minerva Café/Shops**	32 Orwell St, PP
69	**St James House**	12A Springfield Ave, PP
70	**Cahors**	117 Macleay St, PP
71	**Franconia**	123 Macleay St, PP
72	**Piccadilly Hotel**	171 Victoria St, PP
73	**Bernley Building**	15 Springfield Ave, PP
3	**Ithaca Gardens**	12 Ithaca Rd, EB
4	**Elizabeth Gardens**	1 Holdsworth Ave EB
5	**Bayview**	41-49 Roslyn Gardens, PP
6	**Tor**	51 Roslyn Gardens, PP
7	**76 Roslyn Gardens**	76 Roslyn Gardens, EB
8	**Aquarius**	50 Roslyn Gardens, EB
9	**Ercildoune**	85 Elizabeth Bay Rd, EB
10	**Murrawan Court**	3 Elizabeth Bay Cr, EB
11	**Oceana**	108 Elizabeth Bay Rd, EB
12	**Riviera**	106 Elizabeth Bay Rd, EB
13	**Ashleigh**	104 Elizabeth Bay Rd, EB
14	**International Lodge**	100 Eliz Bay Rd, EB
15	**Brentwood Gardens**	90 Eliz Bay Rd, EB
16	**Karingal**	3-5 The Esplanade EB
17	**Elizabeth Bay Gardens**	15 Onslow Ave, EB
18	**Macleay Gardens**	8 Macleay St, PP
19	**Chimes**	45 Macleay St, PP
20	**20A Wylde St**	20A Wylde St, PP
21	**Kuttabul**	18 Wylde St, PP
22	**Gweedore**	12 Wylde St, PP
23	**Fairhaven**	8 Wylde St. PP
24	**The Gateway**	3 Wylde St, PP
25	**Denison**	15 Wylde St, PP
26	**Serendipity**	3-5 St Neot Ave, PP
27	**Gemini**	40 Victoria St, PP
28	**Habitat**	1 MacDonald St PP
29	**St Vincent's College**	1 Challis Ave, PP
30	**The Macleay**	28 Macleay St, PP
31	**40 Macleay St**	40 Macleay St, PP
32	**El Alamein Fountain**	Macleay St, PP

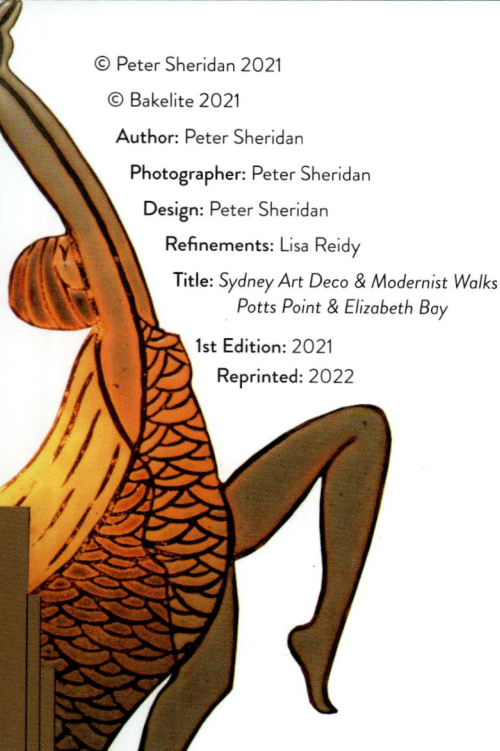

© Peter Sheridan 2021

© Bakelite 2021

Author: Peter Sheridan

Photographer: Peter Sheridan

Design: Peter Sheridan

Refinements: Lisa Reidy

Title: *Sydney Art Deco & Modernist Walks
Potts Point & Elizabeth Bay*

1st Edition: 2021
Reprinted: 2022

All rights reserved. No part of this work may be reproduced or used in any form or by any means – graphic, electronic or mechanical, including photocopying, scanning, information storage or retrieval systems – without written permission from the author. Every effort has been made to source and credit images as well as contacting copyright owners.

ISBN: 978-0-9923896-1-1

A catalogue record for this book is available from the National Library of Australia

Proudly supported by

ART DECO AND
MODERNISM SOCIETY
OF AUSTRALIA INC.

SYDNEY
Art Deco & Modernist
POTTS POINT & ELIZABETH BAY
WALKS

Peter Sheridan AM

CONTENTS

View of Potts Point/Elizabeth Bay from the harbour at Elizabeth Bay

MAP & LISTING	Inside Cover
ABOUT THE WALK	8
GETTING THERE	11
LOCAL HISTORY	12
THE NEIGHBOURHOOD	14
RENTING OR OWNING A FLAT	16
ARCHITECTURAL STYLES	18
ART DECO	19
MODERNIST	26
IMPORTANT ARCHITECTS	28
THE WALK STARTS HERE	**34**
INDEX	192

Macleay St, Potts Point 2020

The 'Parisienne' end of Macleay St looking south towards Kings Cross

This book is as much a manifesto as a walking guide, validating this small precinct as a national historical treasure, which should be recognised, protected and promoted. This area is not just a collection of 20th century buildings but a clearly defined and preserved slice of Sydney's physical and cultural history. There is more varied heritage architecture in Potts Point and Elizabeth Bay than perhaps in any other place in Australia, ranging from 19th century Colonial mansions and rows of Victorian terraces

Foreground: Art Deco Macleay Regis (left) and Modernist Chimes (right)

through to apartment blocks in Arts and Craft and Federation styles from the early 20th century. Then follows the explosion of Art Deco apartment blocks from the 1930s and 40s with a late surge of Modernist buildings in the 1960s. Fortunately there is little recent high-rise in the area so the 19th and 20th century heritage landscape is retained. The history, architecture and cosmopolitan lifestyle make this one of Sydney's special places to live in, to visit and, most importantly, to preserve.

ABOUT THE WALK

Urban exploration is a mindset whereby one looks at a neighbourhood searching for new perspectives. Walking allows time to absorb the essence of a locality and enjoy its special features. In this case we are picking a time frame (late 1920s to 1960s) and highlighting the various iterations of Art Deco and Modernist architecture clustered in this small and accessible area of Sydney.

This booklet is a template to see Potts Point and Elizabeth Bay through a predominantly Art Deco filter. I added the Modernist buildings because many people are interested in the broader topic of 20th century architecture and it would not be feasible to do a separate publication about the Modernist buildings in the area although they are an excellent concentrated representation of the period, the style and important architects. The booklet is full of images, background information and specific details regarding individual buildings that can enhance the experience and help the explorer bring into sharper focus each building's design highlights.

The notion for specific locality-based heritage walking booklets came from the success of my book *Sydney Art Deco* which was released in 2019 and reprinted in 2021. Additionally, every time I have been asked to conduct a walking tour of Potts Point/Elizabeth Bay it has been enthusiastically oversubscribed and happily confirms that my love of this area and its Art Deco and Modernist heritage is shared by many Sydneysiders and visitors.

In *Sydney Art Deco* 60 pages were allotted to the PP/EB area and some 30 buildings were featured. In this 200-page walking booklet I have extended the number of buildings to 75 in order to show the full complement of Art Deco buildings in the precinct. As well there are included over 30 Modernist buildings from the 1960s.

While a book may be old fashioned to some, I like the permanence and feel of paper with words and images on the pages. Nevertheless I hope this booklet might be a precursor and sibling to an internet-based version in the near future as well as the foundation of a comprehensive searchable database of Sydney's Art Deco and Modernist buildings. Additionally there are plans to do walking booklets dedicated to the Art Deco of Sydney's Central Business District and perhaps one doing an extended pub crawl of Sydney's amazing Art Deco hotels and pubs.

The map at the front of the book identifies all the Art Deco and Modernist buildings in this area with coloured numbered circles and squares which are also listed with addresses on **the legend** to the right of the map and cross-referenced again on the page describing the building and in the index. The map outlines a suggested route and this will take some 2-3 hours. If time is limited, a short walk up and down Macleay St and then down the steps to Billyard Ave and to Beare Park will provide a good sampling.

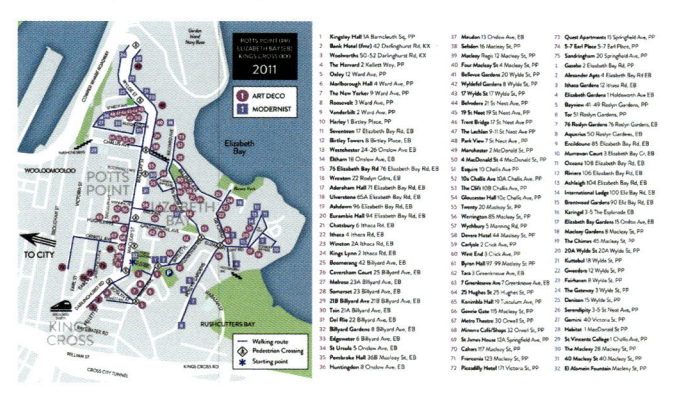

Descriptors for Art Deco buildings are numbered with a purple circle. The important buildings are marked with white numbers, whereas those which can be bypassed because they are modest, difficult to see, require a detour or can be seen from a distance are marked on the map and in the book with black numbers.

Modernist buildings are marked with a blue square and white numbers.

Note: Many buildings are more easily seen in winter months (May to October) when the deciduous trees that line many of the neighbourhood streets have shed their leaves.

Other icons:
→ *Walk this way*　　✱ *Highlight/Take note*
← *Go back*　　🔍 *Look*

ITHACA

CAHORS

Murrawan Court

MINERVA
BUILDING

GETTING THERE

The walk starts at the El Alamein Fountain at the top of Macleay Street, Potts Point.

TRAIN: The El Alamein Fountain is some 5 minutes walk from Kings Cross Station *(see map)* which is on the Eastern Suburbs line.

BUS: The 311 bus, which travels from Central Railway to the City and in reverse, stops in Macleay St within a few metres of the fountain. Check NSW Transport for timetables and routes.

TAXI: A taxi or Uber from the city is approx AU$12.00.

WALK: Walking from the city takes about 20 minutes. The two main routes are:

1. Via William St to the Coke sign and then left onto Darlinghurst Rd which becomes Macleay St.

2. From Macquarie St through the Botanical Gardens or The Domain and down the steps past the Art Gallery of NSW to Cowper Wharf Rd in Woolloomooloo. Walk past the Finger Wharf and then up McElhone Stairs to Victoria Rd. Challis Ave is almost opposite and thence to lights at Macleay St. Turn right and walk to the El Alamein Fountain.

DRIVE: Street parking in the area is always difficult and usually a maximum of 1-2 hours. There is a Parking Station in Ward Ave *(see map)* which is just a 2 minute walk across Fitzroy Gardens past the Police Station to the fountain.

TOILETS: Toilets are behind the El Alamein Fountain next to the Police Station, and in Beare Park.

REFRESHMENTS are available in the many coffee shops and convenience stores along the route.

LOCAL HISTORY

We cannot discuss this area as if it appeared out of nothing 230 years ago when the First Fleet arrived. The indigenous peoples had some 50,000 years of history and culture in this place before this time and in 1788 there were some 1500 local inhabitants of the Eora Nation in the Sydney area when 1200 convicts and marines landed. From that time this area has had an interesting history. Briefly a native village, the Potts Point/Elizabeth Bay area became one of Sydney's first suburbs and, if not the oldest, then definitely the first exclusive suburb from the 1830s to the 1890s with an array of Colonial villas and mansions.

In 1809 Colonel William Patterson granted 30 acres of land to Patrick Walsh, a convict who arrived from Ireland in 1801. He lived here at Paddy's Point until the early 1820s during which time he cleared part of the land and erected fences and a hut.

In 1822 Patrick Walsh's land grant was revoked. Governor Macquarie established the Cove as a native village building huts for the indigenous people at Paddy's Point and provided a fishing boat, fishing tackle and salt and casks to salt fish. He gave the village the name of Elizabeth Town, in honour of his wife.

After the indigenous people had disappeared from the area, Governor Brisbane decided on Potts Point as the site for an asylum. Nothing came of this plan and then Elizabeth Town was granted to important public servants in the Colony who were encouraged to build grand villas. One of the first of these land grants was made to Sir John Wylde, the Judge Advocate in 1822 who was Director of the Bank of NSW. Wylde Street bears his name.

The largest of the grants was made to Alexander Macleay (1767-1848) who was a leading member of the Linnean Society, a fellow of the Royal Society and NSW Colonial Secretary, who received 54 acres in 1826 from Governor Darling. This land grant stretched from the present Macleay Street down to the water's edge from the end of Garden Island to Beare Park. Built at very considerable expense by Macleay, Elizabeth Bay House was once the finest house in the colony, set within a garden of the most remarkable extravagance and fancy. A distinguished entomologist and botanist, his natural history collection was the largest in Australia and formed the basis for the Macleay Collection at The University of Sydney.

Elizabeth Bay House on a small island surrounded by Art Deco apartment buildings.

The Royal Botanic Gardens of Sydney was under his official care in the early days and owes much to him. Unfortunately, Macleay was chronically overstretched and by 1844 he had lost the house. His eldest son, William Sharp, took over his father's liabilities and introduced the family to measures of economy which included the subdivision and sale of most of the Elizabeth Bay property.

In 1830 Joseph Hyde Potts, an accountant to the Bank of New South Wales acquired 64 acres of land from Judge-Advocate John Wylde on what was previously known as Paddy's Point and Woolloomooloo Hill, renaming it Potts Point.

By 1831 17 grants of land had been made on Woolloomooloo Hill to a selection of the most politically and economically powerful men in the colony. The purpose of the grants was to establish a stylish area of housing, and for this reason there were certain provisos on them. Residences were to be erected within 3 years, the house was to cost in excess of £1,000 and had to face Government House across the bay.

Further subdivisions occurred in the 1860s and in the late 1800s, and in the early 1900s significant residential development took place. Eventually, starting in the late 1920s, many of the large mansions and villas were replaced by multi-storey apartment blocks which shaped the precinct as we see it now. Those grand houses that remain have little surrounding land *(see Elizabeth Bay House above)*. Even though the area became much more bohemian, Macleay St was still considered one of Sydney's premiere residential sites. In the 1960s the need for apartments saw more development with Modernist buildings replacing most of the large turn-of-the-century villas on the foreshore.

THE NEIGHBOURHOOD

The walk starts at the El Alamein Fountain just down from the curve where Darlinghurst Road becomes Macleay Street and which also marks the junction of Kings Cross and Potts Point. From here Macleay Street runs south to north down a ridge which defines the area. Potts Point is a thin wedge to the left (west) between Macleay and Victoria Streets , dropping down to the west and south towards the harbour becoming Woolloomooloo. Elizabeth Bay is on the right (east) side of Macleay Street running down to the harbour at Elizabeth Bay and situated between the Navy's Garden Island and Rushcutters Bay.

At the top of Macleay Street is Kings Cross (which is not actually classed as a suburb) and beyond are Darlinghurst and Rushcutters Bay. These suburbs, as well as Potts Point, Elizabeth Bay and Woolloomooloo all share the postcode 2011.

The Potts Point/Elizabeth Bay area is one sq km containing 17000 people and has been for almost a century Australia's most densely populated region. While popular for its restaurants and its proximity to the city and the harbour, it is unique because it contains the greatest cluster in Australia of over 70 Art Deco apartment blocks as well as more than 30 Modernist apartment buildings and nine Colonial villas. This is made more important by the fact that there is a minimum of modern high towers which do not impose or distort the the architectural profile of the area.

In the late 1800s it was a suburb of grand villas; in the 1920s to 1940s living space for people who worked in the city; in the 1950s a centre for bohemians, artists and actors; in the 1970s to 1990s an offshoot of Kings Cross with its nightlife, drugs and organised crime. Today as Kings Cross diminishes both in size and effect, Potts Point and Elizabeth Bay have become desirable places to live.

From the 1920s to the 1940s the number of flats in Sydney increased 6-fold and between 1933 and 1941 over 40% of all the dwellings built in Sydney were flats (mainly for rent) and this area a favoured site at that time for new flat (*or in today's parlance - apartment*) buildings. This gives the area historical charm to add to the vibrance of the local community which is more varied than any other in Australia... ranging from wealthy downsizers to all members of the LGBTQIA+ community, professionals, singles, retirees, backpackers and young marrieds with kids. This hub of Art Deco apartment buildings in a lush tree-lined setting, close to the city and harbour makes the area an unappreciated national treasure akin to Napier in NZ and Miami South Beach in Florida, USA.

Macleay St, Potts Point in the 1940s looking south from the Woolloomooloo end towards Kings Cross at the top. On the left of the street is the Macleay Regis (1938) in the foreground and further up on the left Selsdon (1934), Twenty (1936) and Kingsclere (1912). On the right-hand side is Werrington (1930) and Byron Hall (1928).

RENTING OR OWNING A FLAT

The Potts Point/Elizabeth Bay (PP/EB) area has a completely different demographic and housing profile to the rest of Sydney and Australia. In Australia 90% of people live in houses and 10% in apartments, whereas the reverse is true for PP/EB (i.e. more than 90% live in apartments). 66% of Australians own their own home whereas in PP/EB 60% rent. In fact in the area there are only 29 houses, 386 semi-detached, terrace house or townhouses (mainly in PP) and 288 multi-storey apartment blocks. The bulk of living is in 6000 apartments with an average of 20 apartments per building although this ranges from 5 apartments in a block to some 185 apartments in more modern developments such as the Ikon. The average persons per household in Australia is 2.6 whereas in the Potts Point /Elizabeth Bay area it is 1.5.

For nearly 100 years this area has had the highest density of population in Australia, currently at 17000 people per sq km and yet with minimal high-rise tower buildings. The majority of apartments in the Potts Point/Elizabeth Bay area are 1 bedroom and studios in 2-3 storey walk-up buildings with one and 2 bedroom apartments mainly in 10-12 storey blocks with lifts. Almost all of these were (and many still are) rented. Recently the Melbourne inner city, with a plethora of modern high-rise tower apartment buildings, has taken the mantle of the densest population area in Australia with some 19000 people per sq km.

Owning a property in Australia has, since 1863, utilised a Torrens Title register whereby the purchaser owns both the house and the land on which it is built. By the late 1800s some 44% of Australians owned their own home.

In the 1930s the only way to own a flat was via Company Title (introduced in the USA in the 1880s) where you bought a share in the company that owned the building and were entitled to exclusive occupation of a particular flat in a building on that land. Some of the more upmarket blocks of 10-12 floors with larger apartments, lifts and modern facilities, offered ownership via Company Title. The best examples of these in the Potts Point/Elizabeth Bay area are

Macleay Regis; Cahors; Birtley Towers; Gowrie Gate; Franconia; Meudon; Ashdown ; Caversham Court; Bellevue Gardens; Kanimbla Hall; Mayfair and Byron Hall, all of which still function in the same way today. These buildings reflect the architects' experimentation with this particular style of ownership, extending both the type of accommodation and facilities, and contributing to the diversity of the area's communities. Initiatives towards owner-occupation began shortly after World War 2. One early example was Bolot's 17 Wylde Street which had a slightly different community co-operative title described as 'urban co-operative multi-home units'.

At the beginning of the 1960s Sydney was considered Australia's most modern place to live, mostly because it contained the largest number of flats. Strata title, introduced in Australia in 1961, allows individual ownership of part of a property (called a 'lot' and generally an apartment or townhouse), combined with shared ownership in 'Common Property' (e.g. foyers, driveways, gardens) through a legal entity called the owners corporation. Many of the large Modernist apartment blocks in the area were built in the 1960s reflecting the shift towards high-density high-rise living with the creation of strata titles in 1961. Earlier apartment blocks such 4 Macleay Street in Potts Point (built in 1939 with 50 apartments) was owned by one family and the flats rented out for some 50 years. In 1988 all the apartments were converted to strata title and the majority sold off to individual buyers.

Very few of the Art Deco apartment blocks in the area had garages, exceptions being Macleay Regis, Birtley Towers, Del Rio, Bellevue Gardens, Chatsbury and 17 Wylde St. and in all cases the number of garages were a small fraction of the number of apartments in a building. As the vast majority rented and only 1 in 4 families had a car by 1940, most people relied on the improving standard of public transport (trains, trams, buses and ferries) to get around. The Modernist buildings provided more garages and car spaces adjusting to the boom in car ownership in the 1960s, but with often very limited visitor parking. Even today the average motor vehicles per dwelling in the Potts Point/Elizabeth Bay area is 0.7 compared to NSW overall with 1.7.

ARCHITECTURAL STYLES

The Potts Point/Elizabeth Bay area contains an eclectic mix of 20th century architecture and, from the 19th century, a few mansions and a smattering of Victorian terraces. Unlike most of Sydney's suburbia, there are no Federation houses and Californian bungalows. In most streets there are apartment blocks in Arts and Craft, Art Deco and Modernist styles. Of the 29 houses in the area 9 are 19th century grand villas (*Elizabeth Bay House, Jenner House, Bomera, Tarana, Tusculum, Rockwall, Ashton, Edgerley and Tresco*) and one from the Art Deco period (*Boomerang, 1927*). Most of the Victorian terraces are from the 1870s and are in Potts Point.

Today there are some 300 apartment blocks in the area of which approximately 30% were built between 1928 and 1950 in the Art Deco style. Though many historic buildings have been lost, the Art Deco cluster gives the area its predominant historic flavour and charm. This walking booklet identifies over 70 notable Art Deco apartment blocks and the categories described here show some of the differentiating features of the Inter-War Art Deco buildings plus other architectural styles in the neighbourhood. Because the term 'Art Deco' was not popularised until the 1960s it is a late entrant in architectural terms and in Australia mainly used as one of many sub-categories of Inter-War architecture rather than a style on its own. This is one of the reasons many significant Art Deco buildings in Australia are not listed or heritage protected. Although there are a number of iterations of Art Deco it can be seen as a fundamental foundation of modern 20th century architecture with elements harking back to its classical and Art Nouveau antecedents as well as indicating the streamlined functionalist future that it portended.

Modernist architecture may be in some respects the ultimate expression of Bauhaus principles using modern technology, but there is clearly a transition from the late functionalist Art Deco to the Modernist and seen most dramatically in this area with Bolot's 17 Wylde Street from 1950.

The Modernist buildings have a core shape, utilising similar materials, resulting in a recognisable envelope. The 30 Modernist buildings in the area from the 1960s to 1970s include 5 by Harry Seidler and 6 by Hugo Stossel.

ART DECO

ART DECO can be described as a style, a period, or an accumulation of architectural and decorative shapes. It is often wrapped in a fantasy of a nostalgic world resonating with elegance, excess, cocktails and music.

ART DECO is timeless and boundless....a style that used symmetry, geometric and decorative motifs, curvilinear forms, parallel lines, sharply defined outlines and often bold colours. It is a design aesthetic that spread right round the developed world and impacted on all aspects of life from architecture to theatre and ballet, furniture, jewellery, transport, fashion and typography.

ART DECO as it evolved was a rejection of slavish reverence to the past, looking forward and incorporating speed, the machine age, mass production and new synthetic materials. It held out a promise of modernity and a future for all society that still has relevance today.

ART DECO architecture has a number of variations which reflect both its European and American origins and an extended timeframe between the mid 1920s and early 1950s. They are highlighted by decorative motifs externally on the facade and internally with designs on plaster ceilings and cornices. In the early to mid 1930s there are brick exteriors, often with geometric patterns in the brickwork. Later more streamlined and functionalist examples used white stucco curved facades with little external embellishment.

ART DECO
(1930s)

Art Deco architecture in Sydney highlighted the dynamic aspects of the machine age and modern technology, incorporating modern materials such as terracotta, stucco, reinforced concrete, plywood, chromium-plated steel, coloured opaque glass and textured bricks.

Characteristics: Symmetry and combinations of straight lines – often 3 in parallel – used horizontally, vertically and diagonally in conjunction with geometric shapes (circles, curves, triangles, sunbursts etc). Vertical and horizontal fins were popular in commercial buildings, hotels and cinemas. Much of the exterior ornamentation in apartment blocks was achieved within the brickwork.

Examples: Birtley Towers, PP; Macleay Regis, PP; Adereham Hall, EB; Wychbury, PP; Kingsley Hall, PP;

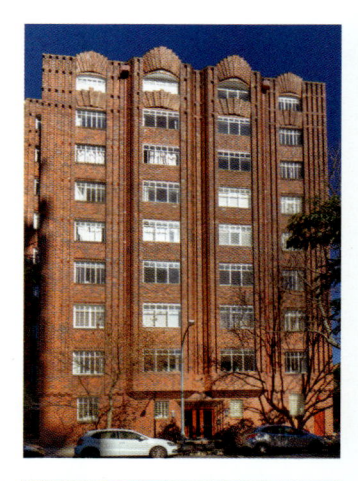

ART DECO FUNCTIONALIST
(late 1930s and 1940s)

A late type of Art Deco architecture and in essence an Australian version of Streamlined Moderne or Art Moderne, where function was more important than style. Ornamentation was either eliminated or integrated. Seen in commercial, industrial, civic, institutional and residential buildings.

Characteristics: Curving forms, long horizontal lines emphasising windows. Sometimes including nautical elements and porthole windows (called P & O style). Plain surfaces, flat roofs, asymmetrical designs incorporating a mix of geometrical shapes such as rounded corners, to give a streamlined effect, cantilevered balconies, hoods, metal-framed windows and doors, smooth-surfaced wall facings (stucco or render).

Examples: Wyldefel Gardens, PP; Ashdown, EB; 17 Wylde St, PP; Marlborough Hall, PP; Wroxton, EB; Metro Theatre, PP; Winston, EB. EB; 17 Wylde St, PP; Marlborough Hall, PP; Wroxton, EB; Metro Theatre, PP; Winston, EB.

ART DECO/
SPANISH MISSION & MEDITERRANEAN REVIVAL
(late 1920s and early 1930s)

Both closely related styles, Spanish Mission had its origins in the Spanish colonisation of Southern California whereas Mediterranean Revival is based on the domestic architecture of Spain and Italy which enjoy a similar climate to Sydney. Often with Art Deco motifs and decorative elements internally.

Characteristics: Generally single or double storey; light tones and colours with wall surfaces usually stucco or colour-washed brickwork, arches, porches, balconies and colonnades. Also terracotta roofing/capping and twisted support columns.

Examples: Bellevue Gardens, PP; Del Rio PP; Boomerang, EB.

ART DECO/STRIPPED CLASSICAL
(late 1920s early 1930s)

Modern ethos with classical design elements but usually smaller scale and without ornamentation.

Characteristics: Symmetrical classical design but with pediments, porticoes, columns and colonnades removed or modified to give an impression of simplicity and plainness.

Examples: Ithaca, EB.

INTER-WAR NEO-GOTHIC/ CHICAGOESQUE/FREE CLASSICAL/BEAUX ARTS
(late 1920s)

Transitional styles combining 20th century elements of construction and symmetry with classical features.

Characteristics: Regular arrangement of building elements with repetitive fenestration; plain wall surfaces constructed of face brickwork or render; classical elements used for emphasis. Often including Art Deco motifs and features internally.

Examples: Franconia, PP; Byron Hall, PP.

SYDNEY CBD

The two major clusters of Art Deco architecture in Sydney are the **Central Business District (CBD)** in the centre of the city extending south from the Harbour Bridge to Central Railway and the **Potts Point/Elizabeth Bay (PP/EB)** area (postcode 2011) some 2km east of the CBD.

The **Potts Point/Elizabeth Bay (PP/EB)** area is approximately one km^2 (100 hectares or 11,000ft^2) so quite small and easy to walk around. Go to page 11 for directions on how to get there and the different modes of transport you can use.

MODERNIST

*MODERNISM arose out of the rebellious mood
at the beginning of the 20th century,
and was a radical approach that yearned to revitalise
the way people viewed life, art, politics and science.*

Flourishing first between 1900 and 1930 it was a rejection of European culture and traditional emphasis on historical cultural influences. The Bauhaus was an art school that was radical in its uniting of art, craft and technology after World War 1. Its main goal was to improve people's living conditions through modern design.

MODERNIST (International style) architecture became prevalent in the 1950s and 1960s was a style based upon new and innovative technologies of construction, such as the use of glass, steel and reinforced concrete. There was the idea that form should follow function (Functionalism) and design would reflect a minimalist mindset with the avoidance of ornament.

Modernist design was implicitly functional, incorporating asymmetrical compositions with the use of geometric forms. Flat roofs were common with the emphasis on horizontal lines. Some of the modern materials used were reinforced concrete, steel frames, curtain walls and ribbon windows. In addition to the minimal ornamentation there was a trend to a white or neutral palette. The interiors (particularly living areas) were open plan and light filled, leading to a feeling of spaciousness.

The early modernist architects were led by Walter Gropius and Ludwig Mies van der Rohe in Germany, Le Corbusier and Robert Mallet-Stevens in France, and Konstantin Melnikov in the Soviet Union. They aimed to emphasise forms and eliminate any kind of decoration.

Harry Seidler and Robin Boyd are considered to be the most highly influential Australian Modernist architects. Boyd worked mainly in Melbourne and designed houses whereas Seidler was Sydney based and his designs covered houses, apartment blocks and commercial buildings.

MODERNIST / INTERNATIONAL STYLE (1950-1969)

Based on Bauhaus principles that form should follow function and a minimalist approach eschewing ornament and decoration. Utilised new and innovative technologies of construction, particularly the use of glass, steel, and reinforced concrete.

Characteristics: Clean lines with repetitive elements (windows, balconies etc); the use of simple building materials particularly reinforced concrete; flat roofs; lots of glass with a focus on natural light; a neutral palette such as white and creams.

Examples: Gazebo, EB; Ithaca Gardens, EB; International Lodge, EB; Oceana, EB; Aquarius, EB; Bayview, EB.

IMPORTANT ARCHITECTS IN POTTS POINT/ ELIZABETH BAY

This walking booklet displays the PP/EB area through the prism of architecture, highlighting examples from two different periods of style in the 20th century. It is important to recognise that taste is fickle and in the case of architecture it is mediated by money, fashion, location, circumstances and politics. The future is always retarded by the obduracy of the status quo and heritage is always in jeopardy from ignorance, opportunism and greed.

Fostering change and innovation in Australia is a relatively modern concept and one has to see the incorporation of Art Deco and Modernist architecture into the locally built environment as individually driven by exceptional and motivated individuals (primarily architects), who often had to battle entrenched views and a staid bureaucracy to change the landscape. At the other end of this spectrum is the pervasive lack of appreciation and commitment to preserving original and novel examples of old architecture, coupled with a particular mindset in NSW that anything can be justified and any old building (regardless of its heritage value) defaced or demolished in the name of progress and adaptive re-use.

While there seems to be a growing reverence for 19th century buildings in Sydney, there is little concern for 20th century buildings which are not well defined, almost never comprehensively documented and generally ignored in State and Council future blueprints. It is interesting that the list of buildings in this book is the first complete listing of Art Deco and Modernist buildings in this neighbourhood and required significant research by the author (with the aid of archivists at Sydney Council) to identify original details. And this brings up the point that it is not only the architecture that is important but the need to also recognise and respect the men and women who conceived and completed these works of art.

Art Deco is an important design aesthetic because it spread globally into countries such as Australia which in the first part of the 20th century was predominantly British in its outlook. As the century progressed better communication and easier travel allowed quicker transmission of new ideas and approaches to architecture and design to reach Australia. The influence of émigré architects is also important as they brought a different cosmopolitan ethos as well as their direct connections with the new design schools of Europe and America.

Two of the most important architects in Australian architecture of the 20th century are prominently represented in the Potts Point/Elizabeth Bay area - Emil Sodersten with 5 Art Deco masterpieces and Harry Seidler with 5 Modernist gems. Sodersten is the master of Art Deco showing quite different designs before and after a trip overseas to Europe in the mid 1930s. Seidler brought Bauhaus to Australia through his experience with luminaries such as Gropius, Breuer, Aalto and Niemeyer.

While Sodersten and Seidler are clearly icons of their respective styles, Aaron Bolot and Hugo Stossel both straddled the Deco/Modernist divide. Bolot's 2 buildings in this area highlight his important influence in the evolution of Australian architecture in the mid 20th century with perhaps some of this innovativeness attributed to his time with Walter Burley Griffin and by extension to Frank LLoyd Wright. Stossel, an émigré architect like Seidler, appears at the end of the Art Deco period with St Ursula (5 Onslow Place) but flourishes in the Modernist period of the 1960s with another 6 apartment buildings in the area.

A mention should also be made of Bruce Dellit who designed the Metro Theatre in Potts Point (and the War Memorial in Hyde Park). The Metro is one of the few commercial Art Deco buildings in the area and one of the most important examples of streamlined Art Deco live/movie theatres in Australia. Yet it has only recently been heritage listed and will more than likely be modified into some sort of commercial space, notwithstanding the enormous benefit to the area and Sydney that would accrue from bringing live theatre back to the Metro.

EMIL SODERSTEN

https://en.wikipedia.org/wiki/Emil_Sodersten

EMIL SODERSTEN (1899-1961) was the most productive exponent of the Art Deco style of architecture in Sydney. As well as being the joint architect for the National War Memorial in Canberra he designed many apartment blocks and commercial buildings in Sydney. Between 1931 and 1935, Sodersten explored the dramatic potential of the modern form designing a range of buildings where he manipulated the decorative potential of brickwork with fans, vertical ribs, texture and pattern. The serrated windows in the CML and QBE buildings are a feature of Sodersten's work as is the decorative and intricate brickwork seen in Birtley Towers and Wychbury.

Malborough Hall's modern lines shows the influence of his trip overseas to Europe and America in the mid 1930s where he was influenced by European Modernism.

Sodersten's 5 buildings featured in this book are:
Kingsley Hall (1929), *Werrington* (1930), *Birtley Towers* (1934), *Wychbury* (1934) and *Malborough Hall* (1938).

HARRY SEIDLER

HARRY SEIDLER (1923-2006) was an Austrian-born Australian architect who is considered to be one of the leading exponents of Modernism's methodology in Australia and the first architect to fully express the principles of the Bauhaus in Australia. Seidler studied and worked in Canada and America with luminaries of the design world such as Walter Gropius, Marcel Breuer, Alvar Aalto, Josef Albers and Oscar Niemeyer and his work shows their influences.

Harry Seidler designed a series of apartment blocks in Sydney with expressed concrete frames, balconies (which only became common in the 1950s), brick infill walls and careful attention to sun control, all in the best Modern Movement tradition and imitated by other architects. He also introduced novel innovations such as splitting access to apartments and double-height living rooms overlooked by mezzanines containing bedrooms.

He designed more than 180 buildings and received much recognition for his contribution to architecture of Australia. Many of Seidler's designs were a highly demonstrative enactment of his Modernist design methodology, which he saw as an amalgam of 3 elements: social use, technology and aesthetics.

Seidler's 5 buildings in this book which reflect his period of mastery of reinforced concrete are: *Ithaca Gardens* (1960), *Ercildoune* (1965), *Aquarius* (1965), *Gemini* (1962/1969) and *International Lodge* (1970).

AARON BOLOT

AARON BOLOT (1900-1989) is regarded as an important architect in the history of high-rise design in Australia. Bolot left Crimea with his family in 1911 to resettle in Australia. In 1926 he graduated from Brisbane's Central Technical College where he studied architecture, being awarded the Queensland Institute of Architects Gold Medal. Bolot moved to Sydney in the early 1930s and assisted Walter Burley Griffin on the Pyrmont and Willoughby incinerators in 1933 and 1934. By the late 1930s he was an independent architect specialising in theatres and apartment buildings. His works in Sydney include The Dorchester in Macquarie St (1936), The Ritz Theatre in Randwick (1937) and Hillside Apartments in Edgecliff (1935). As well as designing some country theatres in NSW he redesigned the Melba Theatre in Melbourne, which was renamed the Liberty. From 1941-1946, during World War 2, Bolot served with the Australia Forces overseas.

Ashdown in Elizabeth Bay (1938) is a seminal example of the Functionalist style, built with reinforced concrete and painted 'pure white'. Notable designs after the war include an apartment building at 17 Wylde Street in Potts Point which was completed in 1950 and is his finest work. The building was registered in 1997 with the Register of the National Estate. Bolot's work reflects his skill and understanding of modern architecture as he displayed the best of Art Deco functionalism with Ashdown in 1938 and then segued into one of the first transitional examples of Modernist architecture in Australia with 17 Wylde St in 1950.

In the Potts Point/Elizabeth Bay area Bolot's contributions are: *Ashdown* (1938) and 17 Wylde St (1950).

HUGO STOSSEL

HUGO STOSSEL (1905-2002) was another of the highly skilled and highly educated émigré architects who fled Europe in the late 1930s to escape Nazism. Born in Hungary he trained in Rome and Vienna and had travelled widely in Europe before arriving in Sydney in 1938 aged 34.

Stossel's projects in Europe were featured in architectural magazines there and in the USA. He was initially employed by the NSW Department of Works and Housing and then worked for the architectural firm Cody and Willis. In 1947 he was registered in NSW as an architect and worked mainly in residential homes and apartment blocks around Sydney including Yarranabee Gardens in Darling Point and houses in Wahroonga and Warrawee. He also designed the NSW Police Headquarters in College St (1973) and the Airport Hilton Hotel in Mascot (1981).

5 Onslow Avenue is perhaps his most elegant work as well as being a transitional design at the end of the Art Deco era. All the others in this area are clearly in the Modernist style. He was last registered as an architect in NSW in 1991, when he lived in Woollahra, aged 97.

In the Potts Point/Elizabeth Bay area Stossel's 7 buildings include:
5 Onslow Ave (1951), *Elizabeth Gardens* (1960), *Chimes* (1964), *Tor* (1965), *Denison* (1966), *Macleay Gardens* (1967), *Bayview* (1968).

THE WALK STARTS HERE

- 🔍 **Look at Kingsley Hall behind the El Alamein Fountain (which we shall see again at the conclusion of the walk).**
- ✱ **Note the decorative brickwork at the top of the building.**
- ➜ **Go inside Cafe Giorgio at street level to see the original ceiling and lighting details.**

Behind the El Alamein Fountain is **KINGSLEY HALL**, built in 1929 and one of the first Art Deco apartment blocks in the area. It was designed by one of Sydney's most prolific and respected architects of the time, Emil Sodersten.

From some aspects the walls seem like unsupported facades, but this is a substantial brick building. It comprises a 10-storey Art Deco apartment block, constructed with a concrete frame and clad in distinctive red-face textured brickwork with Aztec motifs incorporated within the detailing of the brick parapets.

Kingsley Hall was born into an era of glitz and glamour. By March 1930 there was already a demand for the luxury flats in Kingsley Hall and it was announced that 20% had already been let. The block contained 20 flats and this was described as being 10 years ahead of its time. The planning was arranged so that there were no dark rooms.

The building was designed for professional people, wealthy widows and pastoralists who would come to town for some weeks or months and rent a furnished apartment. Some original internal elements can be seen in Cafe Giorgio on the ground floor including Art Deco style recessed ceilings and light fittings.

KINGSLEY HALL (1929)
1A Elizabeth Bay Rd, Potts Point
Architect: Emil Sodersten

➔ *Walk along Darlinghurst Rd south towards the Coca-Cola sign.*

✱ *Both the Bank Hotel ② and Woolworths ③ are difficult to see and can be left to the end of the walk where they are better viewed from the other side of the road (p185). Both are obscured by foliage, particularly in summer.*

The former **BANK HOTEL** is easily missed, hard to see and in poor repair. The major features are the 3 imposing fluted vertical fins extending out from the very plain front of the building. These are a wonderful example of classic columns (which can be seen on the building next door) evolving into a quintessential Art Deco decorative motif reflecting geometry, angles and parallel lines.

BANK HOTEL (1940)
42 Darlinghurst Rd, Kings Cross — ②

WOOLWORTHS (1939)
50-52 Darlinghurst Rd, Kings Cross
Architects: Mackellar & Partridge

3

Opened in December 1939 as a **WOOLWORTHS** store, this 5 storey Inter-War Art Deco style building housed a retail outlet at street level, the Balcony Cafeteria on its first floor and stores, staff rooms and a kitchen on its other three floors. Its simple modern design incorporated a green-glazed, ceramic-tiled facade and steel and bronze-framed windows and doors.

During World War 2, it housed the Combined Services canteen and, in the post war period, the Australian Broadcasting Corporation leased the 3 upper floors. Today it is home to the Kings Cross Library and Sydney Council.

➜ *Turn left down Roslyn St at the Empire Hotel. Just before you reach Ward Ave turn sharply back to the right up Kellet Lane. The Harvard is at the top on your right.*

THE HARVARD (1935)
2 Kellett Way, Kings Cross
Architects: Summerhayes, Son & Allsop

4

The **HARVARD** is a surprising Art Deco gem from 1935 well hidden in the back streets of Kings Cross. It is a 4-storey brick building with 16 apartments. The major features are the decorative white plaster friezes at the roof line extending down vertically to the entrance doors.

At the top of the building the attractive exterior friezes with repeating chevron shapes meet at the bevelled edge of the building with an elongated sunburst motif pointing down to the elegant vertical typeface of the building's name. Some of the interior architraves, railings and pelmets are also Art Deco inspired.

← *Walk back down Kellet Lane to Ward Ave where you will see Oxley on the opposite corner.*

→ *Alternatively follow Kellet Lane into Kellet St and walk down to Ward Ave past all the Victorian terraces with their iron lacework and ornate decoration, enjoying the mix of modern restaurants and seedy establishments.*

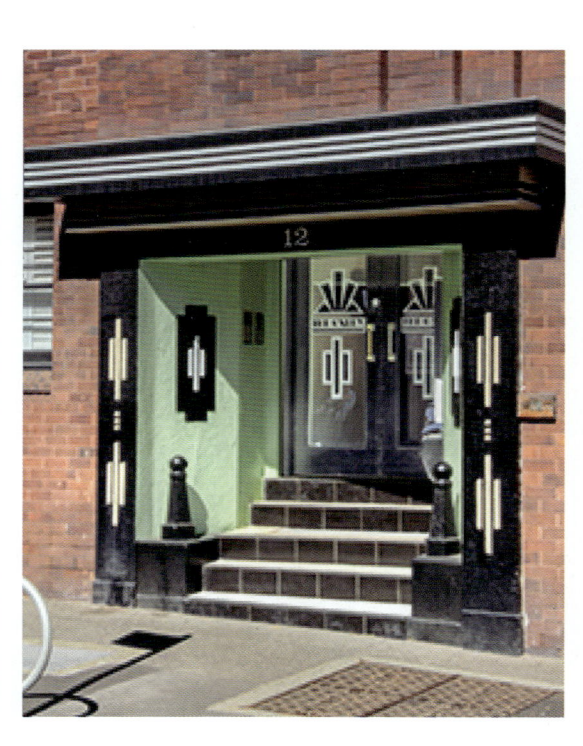

Corner Ward Ave and Roslyn St

The **OXLEY** is one of the area's treasures. It is a smaller 3-storey walk-up apartment block, but contains many Art Deco elements. The colour and contrast of the black, white and green Hollywood style decorative elements at the entrance are matched by the intricate glass signage above the awning using the same colours. The entry steps are white and black tiles, giving a piano keyboard effect.

The brickwork has many Art Deco touches, notable being the stepped brick planters under the windows and the embossed brick squares around the windows on the chamfered corner of the building.

OXLEY (1936)
12 Ward Ave, Potts Point

➜ *Walk east 20m along the left hand side of Ward Ave and Malborough Hall is on the other side of the road.*

MALBOROUGH HALL is an extraordinarily modern looking apartment block for the time, containing 62 apartments which were described at the time as bachelor flats. The L-shaped plan provided most of the apartments with a north-easterly aspect, some with views of the harbour and also included a swimming pool and private gardens.

Sodersten had been to Europe and North America a year earlier and this work reflects his work with European Modernism. The extensive use of mottled brick in horizontal bands and a 6-storey, angled amber glass stairwell facade are indicative of what was then the new Functionalist style.

There is a white rendered canopy awning above the entrance with a smaller duplicate at the top of the tower. Smaller overhangs extending in horizontal bands above the rather tiny windows enhance the appearance of the building.

MARLBOROUGH HALL (1938)
4 Ward Ave, Potts Point
Architect: Emil Sodersten

6

43

Original foyer of Malborough Hall

Sam Hood (Collection State Library of NSW)

← *Behind you on the west side of the road will be The New Yorker and the The Roosevelt .*

→ *Walking some 30m east along Ward Ave you will see The Vanderbilt on the other side of the road.*

These three modest 3 storey apartment blocks close together on Ward Ave are remarkable mainly for the grandeur of their names aspiring to create an image of Manhattan luxury. **THE NEW YORKER** and **THE ROOSEVELT** are close to each other on the west side of Ward Ave and both have similar symmetrical step-back shape with vertical and horizontal elements in the brickwork highlighting a centrally placed doorway.

THE NEW YORKER (1938)
9 Ward Ave, Potts Point
Architect: G N Kenworthy

7

THE ROOSEVELT (1938)
3 Ward Ave, Potts Point
Architect: G N Kenworthy

THE VANDERBILT (1935)
2 Ward Ave, Potts Point
Architect: G N Kenworthy

THE VANDERBILT is a few metres north on the other side of Ward Ave and presents a simple facade as it straddles the curve in the road and a corner site. The plain brickwork is accentuated by a series of parallel horizontal lines between the floors.

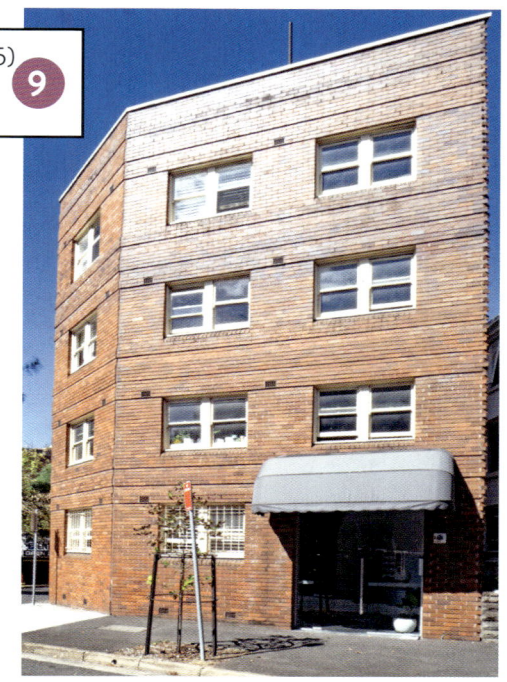

➜ *Stay on the left-hand side of the road and directly ahead of you as Ward Ave curves to become Elizabeth Bay Rd is the Modernist building, The Gazebo, from 1969.*

One of the outstanding Modernist landmarks in Sydney, the **GAZEBO** incorporates a unique 18-storey construction method, determined by its cylindrical shape and has a radiating concrete frame which determines the floor plan design. Many apartments are wedge-shaped which take advantage of wide-panorama vistas.

The Gazebo was originally a hotel and its 1960's Functionalist and funky decor included modern plastic furniture and orange carpet. Its white marble aggregate facade was described at the time as *'one of the most spirited additions to Sydney's skyline for some time'*.

The site includes an adjoining rectangular, complementary apartment block with courtyards behind the main polygon-shaped tower, built in 1982. Both buildings were upgraded to modern strata apartments in 2005.

GAZEBO (1969)
2 Elizabeth Bay Rd, Elizabeth Bay
Design: Design & Construction Consultants

1

➔ *Next door to the Gazebo are the Alexander Apartments built in 1964.*

Built in 1964, **ALEXANDER APARTMENTS** is a 7-storey apartment block with 46 studio apartments.

ALEXANDER APARTMENTS (1964)
4 Elizabeth Bay Rd, Elizabeth Bay
Architects: Lukacs & Gergely

2

➡ *Continue walking down Elizabeth Bay Rd for some 20m and as the road curves to the left you will reach the entrance to Harley.*

HARLEY is a relatively simple looking building with little exterior ornamentation other than a combination of dark and light horizontal brickwork at the base of the six floors. It has 11 apartments with the top floor apartment having an outdoor patio.

Harley's major feature is the entrance, with walls made of Vitrolite glass panels. This appears to be the only example of Vitrolite in this area, and is unusual in that the structural glass is retained in beautiful original condition and with three different colours. As well, there is a full-width plaster frieze with many Art Deco motifs above the chrome and gloss-black entrance doors.

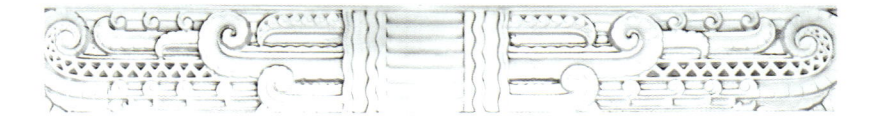

HARLEY (1935)
1 Birtley Place, Potts Point
Architect: Neville J Coulter

10

✱ *Directly opposite on the other side of the road is Seventeen.*

SEVENTEEN is a 6-storey building with 53 apartments ranging from one to 3 bedrooms. The stepped arrangement of the front facade brickwork creates a distinctive streetscape and follows the contour and curve of the road. The horizontal lines of lighter coloured brick add to the aesthetic harmony of the building's frontage. This is also a good example of a building where the Art Deco features are limited to the front of the block and the remainder appears externally to be a brick box with very little in distinctive design and decorative features.

SEVENTEEN (1937)
17 Elizabeth Bay Rd, Elizabeth Bay — 11

➔ *Keep to the left and walk up Birtley Place to the entrance of Birtley Towers. There is no public access to the property and the aspect from the gate only gives a limited view of this beautiful building. Upper storeys can be seen from other vantage points in the neighbourhood.*

BIRTLEY TOWERS (1934)
8 Birtley Place, Potts Point
Architect: Emil Sodersten

12

BIRTLEY TOWERS is a nine storey Inter-War Art Deco style residential flat building, an adaptation of the American skyscraper style to Australian apartment design. It was the largest apartment block in Australia when completed in 1934 and the first after the Depression eased. The building contains 54 apartments on 9 floors with only 14 car spaces. It is considered as one of the highpoints of Art Deco residential architecture in Australia.

Birtley Towers was designed by the prolific Sydney architect, Emil Sodersten, who worked briefly in the office of Walter Burley Griffin (designer of Canberra). Sodersten's influence shows in the highly-textured surfaces with the face brickwork graded from darker shades at the base to light shades at the top. The foyer has been maintained with its elaborate Art Deco detailing, particularly the ceiling and the amber glasswork. The grand port cochère and imposing harbour aspect give Birtley Towers a commanding position in Elizabeth Bay.

Entrance foyer of Birtley Towers

Brickwork detail on upper floors

Roof and upper floors of Birtley Towers

← *Go back down to Elizabeth Bay Rd*

→ *Turn left and continue down the hill to the roundabout where Greenknowe Ave meets Elizabeth Bay Rd, the latter turning to the right down the hill.*

✱ *Opposite is one-way Onslow Ave and the third building on the right from the corner is Westchester. This building has a sort of tudor/deco front but in a few minutes the back of the building (see right) will be seen to be much more in the Functionalist Art Deco style.*

WESTCHESTER (1939)
24-26 Onslow Ave., Elizabeth Bay ⓵⓷
Architects: Crane & Scott

Rear of Westchester seen from Ithaca Ave

WESTCHESTER is a seven storey block with 32 one and two-bedroom apartments and a penthouse on the top floor which has an open garden area and expansive views of the harbour. While the front view has a more neo-gothic or tudor expression with some deco features, the rear view of the building from Ithaca Rd, *(see when standing in front of Chatsbury p82)*, shows a much more modern styling with a vertical bank of curved open verandahs.

➜ *Head down Onslow Ave on the right-hand side for about 20m and you will be in front of Eltham. From the front it is very unassuming, but check out the perspective at the rounded corner of the building.*

← *When finished turn back and head down Elizabeth Bay Rd to the corner of Ithaca Rd.*

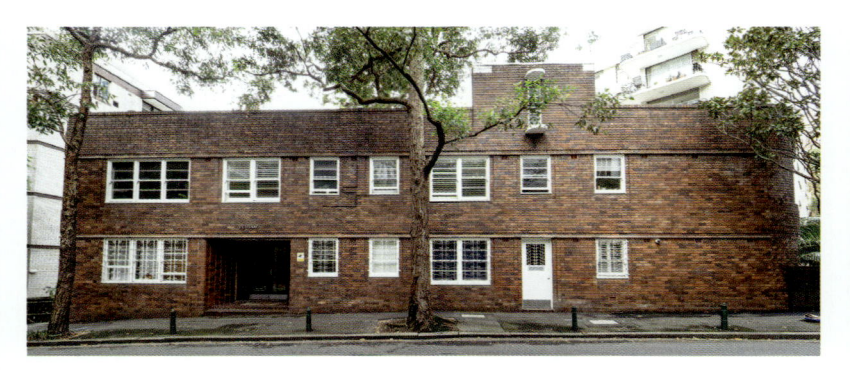

From the front **ELTHAM** appears a rather plain 2-storey building in variegated dark brick, but looking down the south-eastern side one sees a very elegant undulating curve of windows and verandahs as the land drops away and reveals further levels.

ELTHAM (1940)
18 Onslow Ave., Elizabeth Bay

14

🔍 *On the corner of Elizabeth Bay Rd and Ithaca Ave you can see the corner commercial building which although quite a modest 3-storey building has quite interesting deco motifs in the brickwork.*

✱ *A good place to get a drink or snack.*

This building on a corner block (Ithaca Road and Elizabeth Bay Road) is a very simple expression of late 1930's Art Deco styling with its main feature the brick motif at the top of the bevelled facade at the corner, the lines then extending horizontally across the sides of the building which show some minor deco motifs. The Elizabeth Bay shops below the awning show little evidence of any original Art Deco styling. Behind in Ithaca Rd is Harry Seidler's famous Modernist style Ithaca Gardens (1960).

76 ELIZABETH BAY RD (1939)
76 Elizabeth Bay Rd, Elizabeth Bay
Architect: Claud Hamilton

15

→ *Just a couple of metres down Ithaca Ave is Modernist Ithaca Gardens which is quite difficult to see and appreciate through the angled metal fence.*

ITHACA GARDENS was Harrry Seidler's first major development, carried out with Dick Dusseldorp and the first of many projects with Lend Lease. It was to contain 40 2-bedroom maisonettes with the bedrooms on a mezannine floor. Seidler was persuaded to make the apartments one level and it finished as a 10-storey building with 40 apartments, all with harbour views.

Harry and Penelope Seidler lived here for 7 years from 1960 and one of their neighbours in the building was Rupert Murdoch.

The cantilevered canopy over the entrance was unique for the time and became a common element in Modernist apartment buildings in Sydney.

ITHACA GARDENS (1960)
12 Ithaca Rd, Elizabeth Bay
Architect: Harry Seidler

3

➜ *On the other side of Elizabeth Bay Rd is Holdsworth Ave which goes downhill to the steps to Rushcutters Bay Park. At the bottom of Holdsworth Ave on the left is the back of Elizabeth Gardens.*

➜ *To see the front of Elizabeth Gardens you need to go down the steps into the park, which gives lovely views of the harbour.*

Built in 1960 on an escarpment overlooking Rushcutters Bay Park and Marina, **ELIZABETH GARDENS** has 7-storeys with 33 units. There are 12 one-bedroom units, 19 2-bedroom units, and 2 3-bedroom units. The units facing Rushcutters Bay have balconies overlooking the harbour, while most units at the back facing Holdsworth Avenue have urban views.

ELIZABETH GARDENS (1960)
1 Holdsworth Ave, Elizabeth Bay
Architect: Hugo Stossel

4

← *Walk back to the corner of Holdsworth Ave and Elizabeth Bay Rd and a few metres to your left is the corner of Roslyn Gardens.*

→ *Go down Roslyn Gardens about 50 metres till you reach Wroxton on your left*

WROXTON (1936)
22 Roslyn Gardens, Elizabeth Bay
Architect: Dudley Ward

Dudley Ward's influential buildings **WROXTON** and Gowrie Gate in Macleay Street, Potts Point (p172) picked up on innovations in public housing in Germany and Holland. Wroxton stands out with its blonde brickwork and curved open verandahs protruding like a modern version of medieval battlements. There are also smaller motifs like chevron patterns and fretwork in the vertical banks of windows on either side of the balconies. The foyer has recently been restored and original style lights placed on either side of the entrance. The foyer has one of the only terrazzo floors in the area.

➜ *Cross over and continue down Roslyn St on the right-hand side past a lovely row of Paddington terraces on the right hand side.*

🔎 *At the roundabout with Waratah St you will see on the right Modernist Bayview and Tor a little further along on the same side.*

Row of Victorian filigree style terraces c1888. They are constructed of rendered masonry with decorative mouldings and 2-storey front verandah structure embellished by lacework. The front fences are cast iron palisade style with fleur-de-lis spear pickets

BAYVIEW is a large 11-storey, blonde brick block of 110 apartments. It is a large V-shaped building looking directly over Elizabeth Bay, hence its name, Bayview. The apartments feature ceiling to floor windows enhancing the panorama and allowing natural light and ventilation.

BAYVIEW (1968)
41-49 Roslyn Gardens, Elizabeth Bay
Architect: Hugo Stossel

5

TOR (1965)
51 Roslyn Gardens, Elizabeth Bay
Architect: Hugo Stossel

→ *Walk another 50m along Roslyn St and on the east side is 76 Roslyn St.*

← *Come back north along the east side till you reach Aquarius at 50 Roslyn Gardens.*

76 ROSLYN GARDENS (1964)
76 Roslyn Gardens, Elizabeth Bay
Architect: Douglas B Snelling

7

AQUARIUS is an other of Harry Seidler's apartment blocks in the area and perhaps one of the most complete in terms of design and harmony. It was originally called Rushcutters Bay Apartments. It is entered via a curving walkway from the Roslyn Gardens some two levels above the base of the building and the car parking area. The blue shutters on northeastern side are also seen as a feature on Seidler's Gemini Apartments in Potts Point.

AQUARIUS (1965)
50 Roslyn Gardens, Elizabeth Bay
Architect: Harry Seidler & Associates

67

68 ← *Go back along Roslyn Gardens to Elizabeth Bay Rd Head along the right-hand side east into 'The Loop'.*
→ *After about 50m you will find Adereham Hall and behind it Ulverstone.*

ADEREHAM HALL sits on the edge of Macleay Reserve which was the eastern 'wood walk' of Macleay Estate, granted to Colonial Secretary and horticultural enthusiast Alexander Macleay in 1828. Nicknamed 'Gotham City' by locals, Adereham Hall is a 9-storey, 35 metre high concrete apartment block completed in 1934 and a prominent feature of the local skyline. It originally had 25 apartments and 16 car parks. It is an example of the early Art Deco style with sharp geometric and angular contours and significant Art Deco decorative motifs such as sunbursts and parallel lines. *(see entrance and foyer above and roof detail below).*

Name set into a granite plinth at entrance

ADEREHAM HALL (1934)
71 Elizabeth Bay Rd, Elizabeth Bay
Architect: Gordon McKinnon & Sons

17

➔ *Access to Ulverstone is down the right hand side of Adereham Hall but the entrance may be under reconstruction.*

Hidden behind Adereham Hall, **ULVERSTONE** presents as oddly disproportional with two splayed blocks (one with windows and one blank) extending from a semicircular pivot containing the entrance. This is softened by the elegant cantilevered canopy over the steps to the front door with both sharing a similar curvature tying the sections of the building together. This view masks the building's elegance with is its harmonious relationship to Rushcutters Bay mediated by curved bay windows on each end of the eastern side *(see left)*. Note that there are six floors, with two being below the entrance level on the street side.

View from Rushcutters Bay

ULVERSTONE (c1938)
65A Elizabeth Bay Rd, Elizabeth Bay
Architect: C H Christian

18

→ *Walk along the right-hand side of Elizabeth Bay Rd along 'The Loop' for 20m and Ercildoune will be on your right.*

ERCILDOUNE is another of Harry Seidler's buildings named after the Vvictorian mansion it replaced. There are 2 blocks arranged in an L-shape, with primary outlook to the harbour and sun. The projecting bedrooms are similar to his Aquarius Apartments nearby.

ERCILDOUNE (1966)
85 Elizabeth Bay Rd, Elizabeth Bay
Architect: Harry Seidler & Associates

9

→ *Walk down Elizabeth Bay Crescent next to Ercildoune which will give you a view of the back section and second block of Ercildoune.*

✱ *In the cul de sac you can see the entrance to Murrawan Court and the wonderful typeface of the signage.*

MURRAWAN COURT has two completely different facades. The entrance via Elizabeth Bay Crescent is dominated by the car park, but the real essence of the building is seen from the harbour side.

View of Murrawan Court from Rushcutters Bay Park

MURRAWAN COURT (c1961)
3 Elizabeth Bay Cr, Elizabeth Bay
Architect: A Kann

10

➔ *At the top of 'The Loop' is just a hint of the entrance to Tresco (1883) and then the rear views of 3 Modernist buildings - Oceana, Riviera and then Ashleigh, which we will see again from the front in Beare Park a little later in the walk.*

OCEANA (1960)
108 Elizabeth Bay Rd,
Elizabeth Bay

11

RIVIERA (1965)
106 Elizabeth Bay Rd,
Elizabeth Bay
Architect: F.E. Hoffer

12

ASHLEIGH (1973)
104 Elizabeth Bay Rd, Elizabeth Bay
Architect: Ervin Mahrer & Assoc.

13

➜ *Just past Ashleigh on the walk back along the other side of 'The Loop' is Ashton (1875), another of the 19th century villas in the area.*

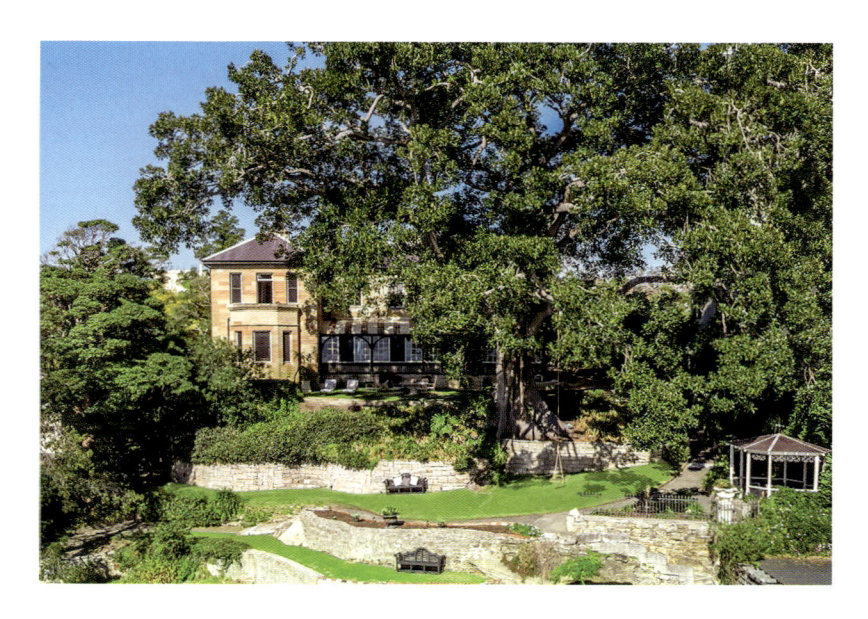

Both Tresco (1883) above and Ashton (1875) below are Victorian Italianate Villas designed by Thomas Rowe.

➔ *One building along is Harry Seidler's Modernist International Lodge and the last built of his apartment blocks in the area.*

✱ *There is a nice trifecta of architecture here with Victorian villa Ashton on the right and Art Deco Ashdown on the left.*

Rear view with Block A in the background and the stepped levels of Block B in the foreground.

INTERNATIONAL LODGE (originally called Ling Apartments) was designed in 1968 and finished in 1970. Seidler's original design for was for 62 small apartments and 2 large 'owners residences' on a single title. The one bedrooms are 40m^2 and the studios 29m^2. International Lodge comprises two buildings. Block A is an 8-storey tower fronting Elizabeth Bay Road with a rooftop terrace. Block B is a 6-storey stepped building which follows the steeply sloping contours of the western part of the site and has a swimming pool at the top.

INTERNATIONAL LODGE (1970)
100 Elizabeth Bay Rd, Elizabeth Bay
Architect: Harry Seidler & Associates

14

→ *Next door to International Lodge is Aaron Bolot's Ashdown with its simple clean white lines and Functionalist curves.*

ASHDOWN (c1938)
96 Elizabeth Bay Rd, Elizabeth Bay
Architect: Aaron Bolot

19

Often described as in the P & O maritime style, **ASHDOWN** is perhaps a better example of European Modernism or Functionalist Art Deco. It exhibits a bold curved bay at the front, planar wall surfaces, metal framed windows in horizontal bands and a flat roof. The two entrances on the side of the building *(see below)* have awnings and flanking elements which are delicately curved and the simple white colour scheme is still chic and elegant today. With no lift, the climb to the top floors is a challenge.

Bolot also designed 17 Wylde Street in Potts Point some 10 years later *(see p126)* which shows his evolution towards Modernist architecture while still retaining his clean and eclectic style.

→ *A couple of steps and you reach Eurambie Hall and next door is Brentwood Gardens.*

EURAMBIE HALL is a narrow strata titled building of 14 one-bedroom apartments which has a spacious common roof-top that offers district views. The entrance has a small Art Deco style semicircular cantilevered portico and vertical brick elements extending toward the roof. *Eurambie* was one of the Aboriginal names for nearby Darling Point.

Entrance detail

EURAMBIE HALL (c1940)
94 Elizabeth Bay Rd, Elizabeth Bay
Architect: John Reid & Son

20

BRENTWOOD GARDENS was built in 1970 with two separate buildings. The front section visible from the street *(see right)* is a constricted 3-storey brick building built side-on to the street with entrances and narrow verandahs on the north side and a driveway and car parking on the south side. Overall the complex contains 34 studio, one- and 2-bedroom apartments.

View from street

BRENTWOOD GARDENS (1969)
90-92 Elizabeth Bay Rd, Elizabeth Bay
Architect: George Coleman

15

➜ *Continue on to the corner of Ithaca Ave and Elizabeth Bay Rd, turn right into Ithaca Ave and go past Ithaca Gardens (p58) and next door is Chatsbury.*

🔍 *Remember to look over the road to see the Functionalist verandahs at the back of Westchester (p55).*

CHATSBURY is an eclectic block of flats with a little bit of everything. A partially castellated roofline, small semi-circular balconies, curved wings at each end and rectangular sections stepping back into the block give this a unique entrance and a great street presence. Note the unusual lower case typography for the name and particularly the cursive script 's' and the 'y' without a tail (*see right*). It is also worth a look on the left-hand side of the steps at the impossibly steep drive to a basement garage (*see right*).

Unusual signage typeface with castellated features on balcony behind

Steep drive to basement garage

CHATSBURY (1938)
6 Ithaca Rd, Elizabeth Bay

21

➜ *Keep going down Ithaca Ave and you reach Ithaca with its wonderful sign on the front on the left of the entrance.*

✱ *The whole building (as well as Winston p86) is better seen from the other side of the road and you can do this when you finish in Beare Park and come back to go down Billyard Ave.*

ITHACA is one of the earliest apartment blocks in Elizabeth Bay showing classical lines but with early Art Deco elements. The entrance has a cantilevered portico, wood and glass doors, and strong horizontal recessed lines on the facade. The sign on the left of the entrance shows Mayan influence consistent with the incorporation in the late 1920s and early 1930s of motifs of ancient civilisations into modern styling.

ITHACA (1927)
4 Ithaca Rd, Elizabeth Bay
Architect: George Phillip

22

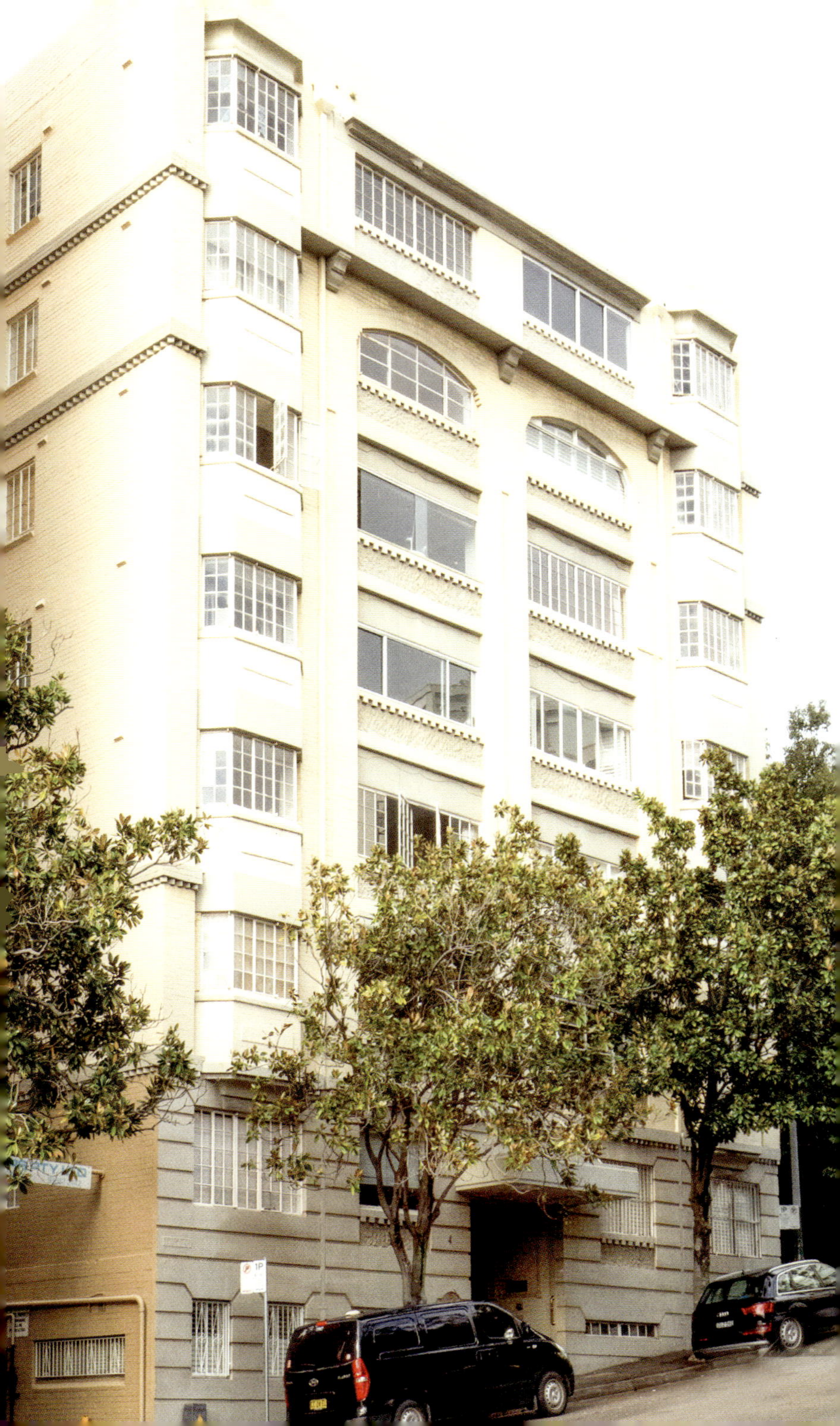

➜ *Winston is just a few metres further down the road and one of the prettiest of the Art Deco buildings in the area with its curved balconies running down the middle of the building.*

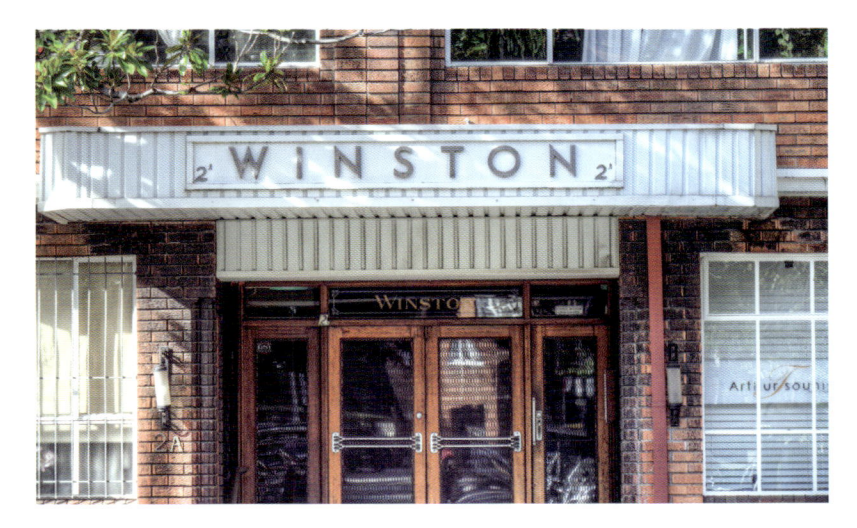

WINSTON is possibly named after Winston Churchill, the famous British Prime Minister. An elegant 9-storey building in the modern functional style with 49 flats. Winston is similar in general design to apartment blocks such Wroxton in Roslyn Street, Elizabeth Bay (see p60), Mont Clair in Darlinghurst and Templeton in Point Piper. However, Winston has the added elegance of curved windows at the corners of the building which capture views and natural light adding a counterpoint to the curved protruding central bank of windows. A nice touch are the blue feature detail tiles in the vertical brick elements. The original balconies have been infilled.

Drawing of Winston from original plans

WINSTON (1940)
2A Ithaca Rd, Elizabeth Bay
Architect: G W Phillips

23

➔ *Next to Winston on the corner facing Beare Park is Kings Lynn.*

KINGS LYNN is a 9-storey block of flats on the corner of Ithaca Rd and the Esplanade with originally 35 one-bedroom apartments. The building has a chamfered profile to accommodate the corner site. The mid-1930s Art Deco facade is rather plain and the windows are all consistent with the original design, not infilled balconies *(see archival photo on right)*. Both Kings Lynne and Winston next door were designed by G W Phillips.

KINGS LYNN (1936)
2 Ithaca Rd, Elizabeth Bay
Architect: G W Phillips

24

Kings Lynn entrance detail

Kings Lynn early 1950s

- ✳ *Beare Park is the perfect spot to relax and have a break and the Lookout Restaurant ideal for coffee or a meal. There are toilets in the restaurant and also in the park.*
- 🔍 *Three Modernist buildings overlook the park...from left to right: Oceana, Riviera and Ashleigh (which you saw from the rear earlier in The Loop). Also there is Karingal in The Esplanade at ground level.*
- 🔍 *There are a group of tall Washington palms near the intersection of Ithaca Road and The Esplanade which are probably remnants from the grounds of Elizabeth Bay House (p109).*

Beare Park & Elizabeth Bay

BEARE PARK is a local treasure, an oasis right on the harbour in the middle of this dense urban environment. There is a walking path along the harbour front and grassy areas for relaxation, and space for children and dogs to play.

In the background are four Modernist apartment blocks. The west side of the park is called Kings Cross Rotary Park and you can see the upper sections of Boomerang (p94) with its pink stucco walls and multicoloured roof tiles.

OCEANA (1961)
108 Elizabeth Bay Rd, Elizabeth Bay
Architect: Theodore Fry

11

RIVIERA (1965)
106 Elizabeth Bay Rd, Elizabeth Bay
Architect: F.E. Hoffer

12

This group of buildings reflect the shift toward high-density living that followed the creation of strata-title ownership in 1961 and the aggressive development of harbour land that once housed gracious houses. Window size and placement in the façade of these buildings reflected the function of the room inside the building. Living rooms had large areas of glass whilst bedrooms and bathrooms often had smaller areas of glass.

OCEANA was one of the first modern, high-rise apartment blocks to appear on the Elizabeth Bay skyline in the early 1960s with seven one-and two-bedroom apartments on each of its 13 floors. Oceana was designed by Theodore Fry (1908-1959) and completed circa. 1961. Fry was another of the émigré architects, coming from Poland in 1948 after World War II, his original name being Teodore Frewillig. Fry completed numerous, multi-storey apartments in the eastern suburbs. An elegant touch of decoration are the closed sections of the verandahs which range from light blue at the top of the building to dark blue on the lower floors.

ASHLEIGH (1973)
104 Elizabeth Bay Rd, Elizabeth Bay
Architect: Ervin Mahrer & Assoc

13

RIVIERA has bed-sitter apartments in the fan-shaped lower section and larger 2 or 3-bedroom apartments in the 8-storey tower section.

ASHLEIGH is a block of 26 units on 13 levels with the main entry on level 6, accessed from Elizabeth Bay Road in the loop (*see p74*). Levels 1-6 each have two 2-bedroom apartments and 7-13 each have 2 3-bedroom apartments.

KARINGAL is an 8-storey building with 80 apartments, made up of 10 bed-sitter apartments on each floor.

KARINGAL (1964)
5-7 The Esplanade, Elizabeth Bay
Architects: Magoffin & Poiner

16

- ← *Walk back to the corner of Billyard Ave and Ithaca Ave and have another look at Ithaca, Winston and Kings Lynn.*
- → *Walk down Billyard Ave on the right-hand side. Most of Boomerang is hidden by high walls but make sure you check out the small door with the boomerang logo.*

BOOMERANG, situated on the harbour in Elizabeth Bay, was designed by English architect Neville Hampson for wealthy Sydney music publisher Frank Albert. The house was built in 1926 in the Mediterranean Revival style (also called Spanish Mission) and is considered one of the oldest and finest examples of the style in Australia. A 3-storey mansion with rendered walls, it has 25 rooms, six bathrooms and four kitchens. A private cinema was constructed in the basement by Albert in 1928 and could seat 200 people.

The name 'Boomerang' relates to the trademark of the Albert family music business which sold Boomerang songbooks and mouth organs. The logo can be seen on the small wooden side entrance to the property as one walks along Billyard Ave. The waterfront land had originally been part of the Macleay Estate of which Elizabeth Bay House (in nearby Onslow Ave) is the only remnant. Frank Albert resided at Boomerang until his death in 1962, after which the house remained closed with a caretaker until 1978. It has recently been faithfully restored to its original splendour and takes its rightful place as one of Sydney's most iconic historic homes.

BOOMERANG (1926)
42 Billyard Ave, Elizabeth Bay
Architect: Neville Hampson

25

95

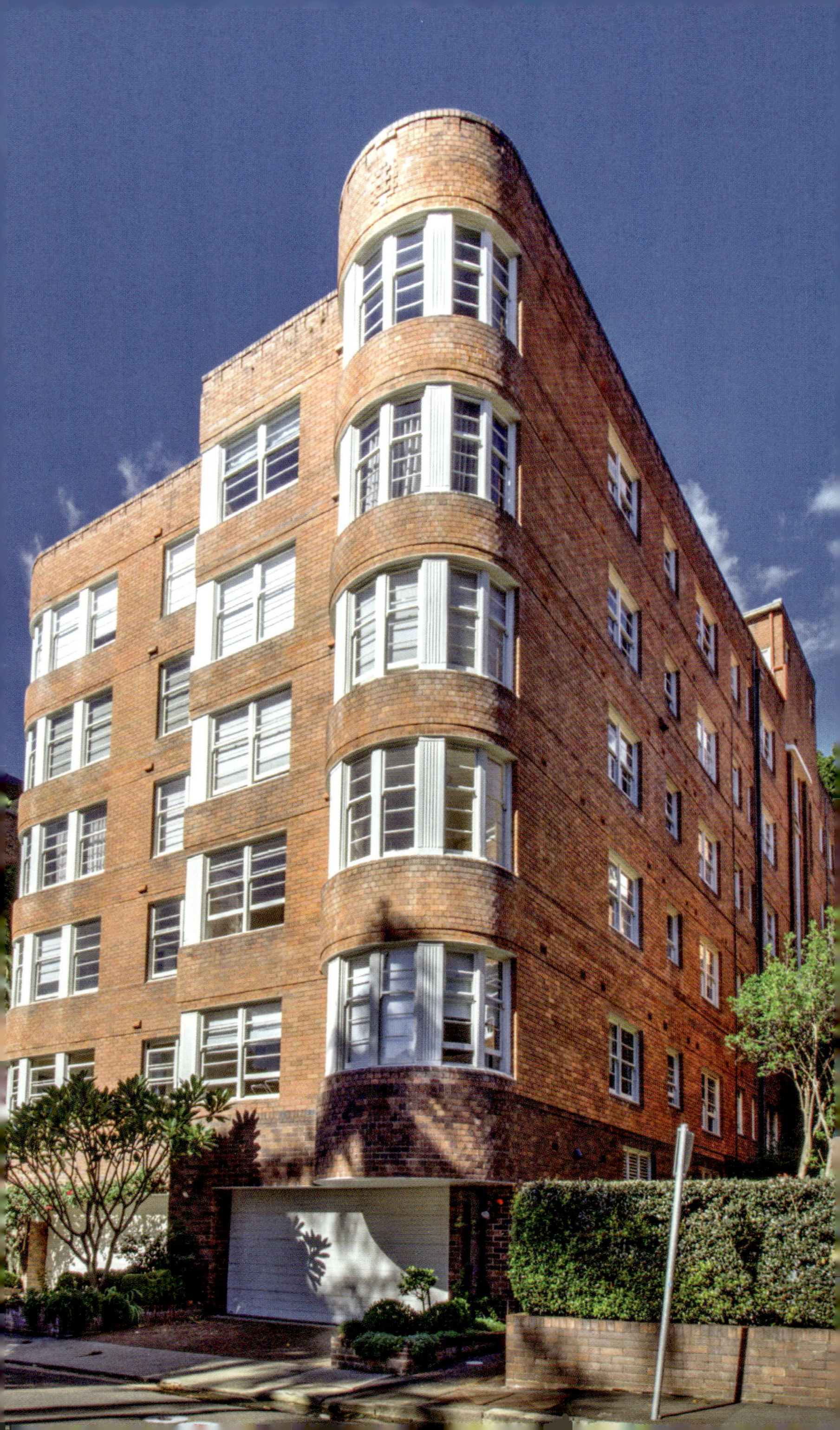

🔍 *On the other side of Billyard Ave is Caversham Court with its elegant curved and stepped front.*

CAVERSHAM COURT is one of a number of apartment blocks in Elizabeth Bay built on what were subdivisions of the gardens of the Macleay Estate. Released in 1927, the block was finally sold in 1934 after the worst of the Depression.

Caversham Court's apartments were on Company Title and intended for the newer wealthy middle class. The shape of the building is clearly Functionalist with curves and horizontal bands of windows. The curved bank of windows at the north-western end give a distinctly nautical flavour to the building and the upper floors providing beautiful harbour views.

CAVERSHAM COURT (1939)
25 Billyard Ave, Elizabeth Bay
Architects: Pitt & Phillips

26

→ *Keep going along Billyard Ave and you will see a series of Art Deco apartment blocks of differing shapes and sizes.*

MELROSE (1942)
23A Billyard Ave, Elizabeth Bay
Architects: Pitt & Phillips

27

SOMERSET (1941)
23 Billyard Ave, Elizabeth Bay
Architects: Pitt & Phillips

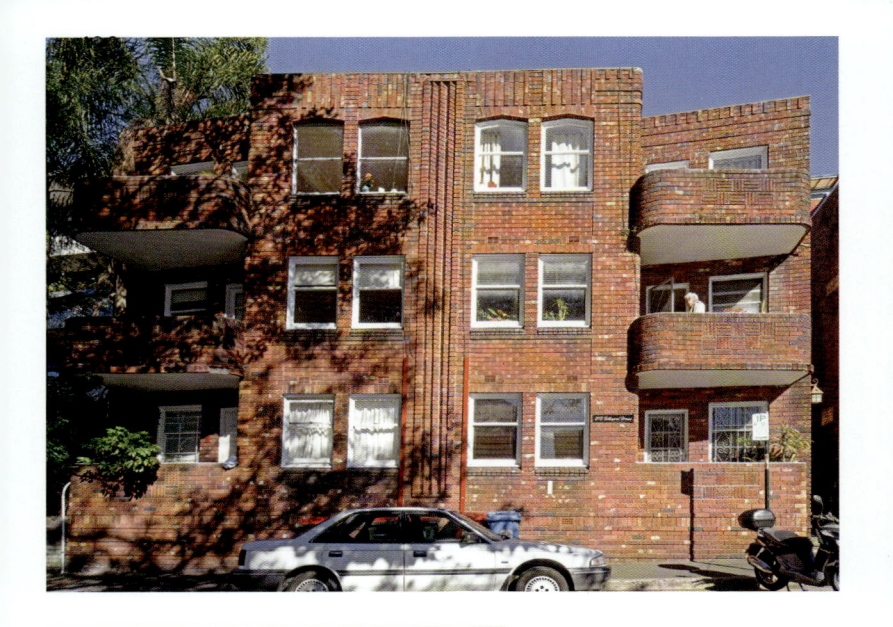

21B BILLYARD AVE (1939)
21B Billyard Ave, Elizabeth Bay

29

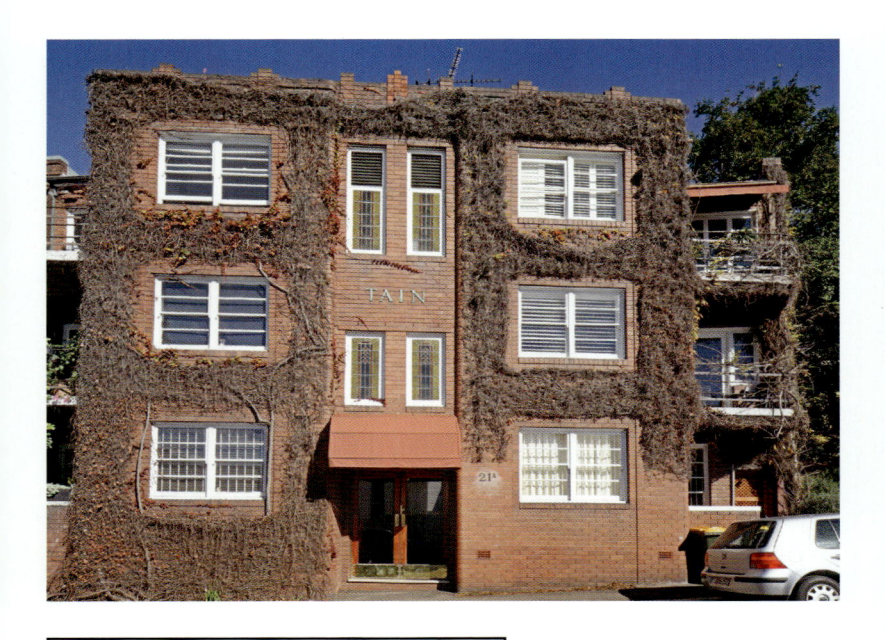

TAIN (1939)
21A Billyard Ave, Elizabeth Bay
Architect: William Tarrant Broome

30

Balconies on Tain facing the harbour

TAIN was part of a 2-block development with the other apartment block (Belltrees) being on Onslow Ave behind and above Tain. Belltrees at 6 Onslow Ave and adjacent to McElhone reserve (*see p110*) was originally to have 20 flats but it has been substantially modified and modernised in recent years. Tain still retains its simple Art Deco facade and contains 6 two-bedroom apartments with lovely bougainvillia overhanging the open verandahs.

➜ *Continuing along Billyard Ave you will see Del Rio on the right on the corner. As Billyard Ave swings to the right you can see just past Del Rio the pink/brown of Edgerley, one of the remaining 19th century villas.*

Designed by John Spencer-Stanfield and built in 1928, **DEL RIO** is an historic Spanish Mission (Mediterranean style) 5-storey block containing five large apartments with Chateau Marmont style arches facing the water. Del Rio overlooks Elizabeth Bay with its lush gardens, jetty and harbour-side swimming pool *(see right)*.

Del Rio means 'by the river or water' and the apartment block straddles the corner of Billyard and Onslow Avenues just below Elizabeth Bay House. It is also just a few doors from the iconic waterfront house 'Boomerang' also built in the Spanish Mission style in 1926.

DEL RIO (1926)
22 Billyard Ave, Elizabeth Bay **31**
Architect: J Spencer Stanfield

Del Rio has large single-floor apartments with shady, deep open verandahs with flagstone flooring. This was an early apartment block for the wealthy, with a garage for each apartment. Wrought iron grillwork on verandahs and doorways adds to the Mediterranean effect.

Early apartment owners names are stencilled in gold lettering on the Spanish style wooden name board in the small foyer. Spencer-Stanfield's firm also designed the Haberfield garden suburb between 1905 and 1914 with all the houses in Federation style.

➡️ *Walk north along Billyard Ave. On the right just before the cul de sac at the end are Edgewater and Billyard Gardens.*

BILLYARD GARDENS (c1940)
8 Billyard Ave, Elizabeth Bay
Architect: E.C. Pitt

Billyard Gardens (left) and Edgewater (right) from Elizabeth Bay

EDGEWATER in its final iteration has 5 storeys, being somewhat smaller and plainer than the proposed 7-storey building in the original plans. In the *Daily Telegraph* of April 1937 Edgewater was described as having 25 soundproof self-contained home units with gardens, swimming pool, tennis courts and a private harbour jetty. Several flats were to be leased furnished in a modern manner with a corner settee facing a large window. Rust curtains and green carpets would blend with the autumn shades of the other furniture.

EDGEWATER (1936)
6 Billyard Ave, Elizabeth Bay
Architects: Morrow & Gordon

33

The Lounge - Dining Room of one of the Furnished Harbour Front Suites. This Furniture has been specially designed and carried out by Murray Bros. Ltd., and is on view at Edgewater to prospective Tenants by arrangement with the Managing Agents.

(Sam Hood (Collection of the State Library of NSW)
Edgewater in 1937 from Elizabeth Bay

EDGEWATER

✱ *To the left at the end of the cul de sac is Macleay Gardens.*

MACLEAY GARDENS is sited at the end of a cul de sac abutting the southern end of the Navy's Garden Island. One of a number of Hugo Stossel designed buildings in the area it is has 8 floors and a mix of apartment sizes: 14 studio, 22 one-bedroom, 6 2-bedroom and a penthouse on the top floor. There is a common flat rooftop with expansive views of the harbour.

One special feature is the rare dual access to the block with a pedestrian entrance to bustling Macleay Street in Potts Point while vehicular entry to the 26 car spaces is via Billyard Ave in Elizabeth Bay.

MACLEAY GARDENS (1967)
8 Macleay St, Potts Point
Architect: Hugo Stossel

17

← *Walk back along Billyard Ave past Del Rio up one way Onslow Ave till you reach Elizabeth Bay House, best seen from the grass verge opposite.*

🔍 *Look at Elizabeth Bay House and the Art Deco buildings behind it.*

✱ *Spend a few minutes enjoying the peace of McElhone Reserve and having a look at the Koi Carp in the lake on both sides of the stone bridge.*

Elizabeth Bay House (1835-1839)

Built at very considerable expense by Alexander Macleay, **ELIZABETH BAY HOUSE** was completed in 1839. It was once the finest house in the colony, set within a garden of the most remarkable extravagance and fancy extending down to and along the harbour front. But Macleay was chronically overstretched and by 1844 he had lost the house.

Further subdivisions occurred in the 1860s and, from the late 1800s into the early 1900s, significant residential development took place. Eventually starting in the late 1920s and through to the 1940s (and again in the 1960s) many of the grand houses were replaced by apartment blocks which shaped the precinct as we see it now.

Real Estate Sale for Elizabeth Bay House 1934

McELHONE RESERVE was originally part of Elizabeth Bay House's lawn area within the carriage loop in front of the mansion. When the property was subdivided and sold in 1927, lots 4, 5 and 6 remained unsold *(see Sales Advert p109)*, and in 1948 they were acquired by Sydney City Council. The garden overlooks Sydney Harbour, featuring lovely lawns and a stone bridge across an ornamental lake filled with koi carp and lilypads. It was designed by Ilmar Berzins, a Latvian immigrant reputed to be Australia's first formally trained landscape architect. The reserve was named after Arthur McElhone, a city alderman for 44 years who died in 1946. It is a lovely spot for locals to picnic and sunbake, for children to play and for wedding photographs.

McElhone Reserve with stone bridge, ornamental lake and Koi Carp

🔍 *To the right of Elizabeth Bay House is 5 Onslow Ave on the corner and behind it is Pembroke Hall in Onslow Place.*

Originally called St Ursula, **5 ONSLOW AVE** is a 6-storey building erected in 1951 and the earliest in the area designed by the well known architect Hugo Stossel. Stossel was a Hungarian immigrant who arrived in Sydney in 1938 and was registered as an architect in 1947. St Ursula is a transitional design between Art Deco and Modernist styles with its gentle curving facade and floor to ceiling windows facing the harbour. It was built from reinforced concrete and steel curtain wall structure with floor to ceiling steel-framed windows. Stossel actually lived for a time in the building which contains a mix of one-, 2- and 3-bedroom apartments.

5 ONSLOW AVE (fmr ST URSULA) (1951)
5 Onslow Ave, Elizabeth Bay
Architect: Hugo Stossel

34

PEMBROKE HALL, built between 1938 and 1940, is a 9-storey building with 22 one-bedroom units and studios. It is only visible from Onslow Place but the main address is in Macleay Street, making it one of the few buildings in Elizabeth Bay with direct access to Potts Point shops and restaurants. The east facing curved verandahs face the harbour and overlook Elizabeth Bay House.

On 21st November 1939 an *"unusual death"* was reported in the media. 50 year-old resident, George Sterling, a Commonwealth Bank bank clerk, still dressed in his pyjamas, fell from the eighth floor roof garden during the night. It is not known how the incident occurred.

PEMBROKE HALL (1938-1940)
36B Macleay St, Elizabeth Bay
Architects: Charles H Christian

→ *Walk along Onslow for a few metres passing the very heavily modified Belltrees and Huntingdon is on your left.*

HUNTINGDON (1939)
8 Onslow Ave, Elizabeth Bay
Architect: W Tarrant Broome

36

➔ *Walk just a little further up Onslow Ave on the left hand side and you will see Meudon and Elizabeth Bay Gardens on the other side.*

MEUDON (1927)
13 Onslow Ave, Elizabeth Bay
Architects: Crane & Scott

37

The imposing **MEUDON** overlooking Elizabeth Bay has similarities to the famous 1902 Flatiron Building on Fifth Avenue in New York, also built on a difficult triangular site. It is a 9-storey apartment building designed in what has been called the Inter-War Free Classical style.

ELIZABETH BAY GARDENS (1970)
15-19 Onslow Ave, Elizabeth Bay
Architect: John Moorcroft

18

ELIZABETH BAY GARDENS is one of the few taller buildings in the area with 15 storeys and 78 apartments.

← Go back along Onslow Ave to the intersection with Billyard Ave.
→ Walk up the stairs from Billyard Ave to Macleay St.
🔍 When you reach the top of the stairs on the flat section you are walking past the rear and side of Selsdon.

➜ *Turn right on reaching Macleay St.*

🔍 *You are now in front of Selsdon which you will see again from the other side of Macleay St later in the walk.*

SELSDON is an ancient English name meaning *'on the hill'*. It was built by Reginald Walker, Bank of NSW Director, whose second wife, Jean, lived in the penthouse. Her name is also still listed on the tenants' notice board. Selsdon includes elements of Old English style, with tracery, gargoyles and heraldic shields. The two pavilions on the roof are Romanesque in inspiration.

> **SELSDON** (1934)
> 16 Macleay St, Potts Point
> *Architects: Prevost & Ruwald*
> **38**

→ *Walk down Macleay St past the local Potts Point Bookshop to the Macleay Regis on your right.*

🔍 *Check out the entrance, the shops on street level and have a look through the doors at the lobby.*

✱ *We will see it again from the other side of the road on the way back.*

MACLEAY REGIS (1939)
12 Macleay St, Potts Point
Architects: Pitt & Phillips

39

MACLEAY
—REGIS

12

The site of the **MACLEAY REGIS** was part of the extensive landscaped grounds of Elizabeth Bay House. Harold Christmas was a major retailer who became one of the founders and the managing director of Woolworths Limited. He bought the land in 1937 and submitted an application to build a block of flats. He set up the Macleay Regis company with seven directors, but in essence the Christmas family owned and ran the building. The Macleay Regis was described in *Decoration & Glass*, April 1939 as '*a mammoth block of luxury flats occupying a commanding position in what is perhaps Sydney's most exclusive residential street and towers nine storeys above the pavement in a most imposing block*'.

One of the last of the grand Art Deco apartment blocks and completed just before the start of the World War 2, Macleay Regis had a New York style and catered for a wealthy clientele. It had 87 apartments and a penthouse. It contained all the modern conveniences such as centralised refrigeration and hot water, elevators, and a kitchen to supply meals to residents. It also included a live-in concierge, a maid service and an internal telephone system that connected occupants to the pharmacy, cobbler, hairdresser and florist located in the small shops on the ground floor at street level.

Macleay Regis in 1939 looking North

Courtesy www.pt.slideshare.net

There were also parking garages for cars (a rarity in the Art Deco buildings in the area). The red brick and the yellow painted woodwork on the windows and balcony doors give a rich but tasteful contrast. The entrance is imposing with a cantilevered awning and a gracious foyer. The curved balconies with their open railings are a special feature of the building and unlike many buildings these have been meticulously retained and maintained.

Curved balconies with open railings

🔍 *Across the road is the Yellow House with its wonderful history and influence on Sydney's art scene in the early 1970s.*

The **YELLOW HOUSE** was an artists collective established by Martin Sharp from 1970 to 1973. The Yellow House Artists Collective included artists such as Brett Whitely, George Gittoes, Peter Weir and Philip Noyce and the work displayed included paintings, sculptures, films etc with the house itself (walls, floors and ceilings) being part of the gallery and performance space. The four sculptural balconies by artist Michael Snape symbolise each of the four elements of earth, water, air and fire. The building adds a wonderful essence of the bohemian ambience that has always been part of Potts Point.

🔍 *Just to the the right of the Yellow House is Chimes with its raised car park to the left of the main building.*

✱ *The rear view of Chimes will be seen a little later in the walk (see p148).*

Another of Hugo Stossell's buildings, **CHIMES** is a 10-storey building with 80 studio apartments. The building sits on less than a third of its 1280 sqm holding.

CHIMES (1964)
45 Macleay St, Potts Point
Architect: Hugo Stossel

19

➜ *Continue down Macleay St a few metres and you will see Four Macleay St with its red brick Art Deco entrance and facade.*

Typical of most apartment blocks from the 1920s to 1940s the whole building was owned by one family and people rented the flats *(which we now call apartments)*. **FOUR MACLEAY STREET** was converted to strata units in the 1980s when the owners sold most of the apartments and part of the land on the harbour side for another apartment block development. Again typically the front is quality brick in the Art Deco style with a cheaper brick and a more amorphous style for the rest of the building.

FOUR MACLEAY STREET (c1938)
4 Macleay St, Potts Point
Architect: William Tarrant Broome

40

➔ *Next door is Jenner House which is difficult to see behind the high wall and opaque gates. Later on you can get a better look at it from the other side of the street.*

JENNER HOUSE is an 1870s Edmund Blacket designed marine villa and one of the last of its type remaining in Sydney. It is also significant because the northern wing is a fine example of servants' quarters and the eastern garden on the harbour side contains the original circular gardens.

Jenner House from harbour aspect. Note Art Deco 4 Macleay St next door and Modernist The Chimes in the background on the other side of Macleay St. On bottom left edge of photo is the heritage listed circular garden.

→ *Continue down Macleay St for 30m as it becomes Wylde St and in front of 20 Wylde St you are opposite the beautiful curved white building which is 17 Wylde St. The back of the building can be seen later when we come up MacDonald St (p149).*

Aaron Bolot was a young Crimean refugee who achieved great success in Australia as an architect, working at one stage with Walter Burley Griffin. He also designed Ashdown in Elizabeth Bay *(p78)* and the Ritz Theatre in Randwick.

17 WYLDE ST was designed in 1948 and finished in 1950. The building was completely unique for its time with no name and being a Community Cooperative title (an early form of strata title). It was one of the first curved buildings in Sydney graciously filling an awkward corner site. The east and north facing facade of glass windows in horizontal bands provide not only harbour panoramas, but natural light, winter sun and natural ventilation for living rooms and bedrooms. Each apartment was designed for easy access, flow and comfort *(see p128)*. Kitchens and bathrooms were sited at the back facing south and west, with small scalloped verandahs.

The very unusual concave shape to the back of the building has a quite different visual impact than the convex curve of the front.

17 WYLDE STREET (1950)
17 Wylde St, Potts Point
Architect: Aaron Bolot

41

The concavity is offset by scalloped verandahs which gives a sense of Bauhaus meets Gaudi but in a coherent and elegant fusion. Sadly only the top of the back of the building can be seen and the totality of Bolot's architectural innovations are not able to be fully appreciated from the street.

The seamless integration of curves and horizontal elements make this building a landmark in the area, one of the great heritage buildings in Australia, and a fitting transition from Art Deco to the Modernist era.

Interior 17 Wylde St 1951 Photo Max Dupain: courtesy State Library of NSW

Top floors at back of 17 Wylde St seen from MacDonald St (p149)

🔍 *From the entrance to 20 Wylde St you can see two Modernist buildings which are currently part of the Navy – 20A Wylde St and Kuttabul.*

20A WYLDE ST (1958)
20A Wylde St, Potts Point
Architects: Havens & Kirkwood

20

HMAS KUTTABUL NEW BARRACKS (1963)
18 Wylde St, Potts Point
Architect: C'wealth of Australia, Dept of Works

21

✱ *The driveway behind you is the entrance to Bellevue Gardens which unfortunately is hidden from public view.*

BELLEVUE GARDENS is a 1927 Spanish Mission style building, unusual in that the entrance to the apartments is via a rooftop carpark. The 8 expansive apartments with high ceilings had views and access to the harbour prior to the expansion of Garden Island in 1940. The famous opera singer Dame Joan Sutherland lived here.

BELLEVUE GARDENS (1927)
20 Wylde St, Potts Point
Architect: Frederick G Deane

42

➜ *Continuing down Wylde St you will see the side view of Gweedore.*

The side view of **GWEEDORE** shows horizontal eyebrows merging with the verandahs for each floor. This is offset by a thin vertical brick element in the centre of the building which one sees elsewhere as the stairs or lift well but here seems to have little purpose but aesthetic. At the front there are green glass sections below the windows which are difficult to appreciate because of the large tree on the footpath.

GWEEDORE (1960)
12 Wylde St, Potts Point
Architect: V Moratelli

22

→ *Just before you reach Fairhaven you will see two of the 19th century Victorian villas, Bomera and Tarana, on the other side of the road. The front of the houses face the harbour.*

Bomera (1856) — Courtesy Domain.com.au

BOMERA was designed by John F. Hilly and built in 1856 for colonial merchant William McQuade. **TARANA** was designed by Edward H. Buchanan and built by John Alexander Oag in 1889, with additions including a third-storey designed by Sheerin & Hennessy in 1907.

Tarana (1889)

➜ *A few metres further down Wylde St on your right is Fairhaven.*

FAIRHAVEN is made up of two blocks connected by a walkway, the smaller Block A closer to the road is 3-storeys and the larger Block B behind, with excellent views over Garden Island to the harbour, is 7 storeys.

FAIRHAVEN (1967)
8 Wylde St, Potts Point
Architect: R Lindsay Little

23

* Next to Fairhaven is the entrance to Wyldefel Gardens which unfortunately is hidden from view.
* You can see a little of the cascading nature of the complex from the drive area of Fairhaven.

WYLDEFEL GARDENS was designed by architect John Brogan and completed in 1936. The 20 apartment complex was built for a prominent art collector, connoisseur and entrepreneur, William Crowle within the gardens of the 1890s Victorian mansion Wyldefel. The 20 apartments were specifically designed to retain views of Sydney Harbour from the house. With its U-shaped layout and stepped down design, where the roof of one apartment becomes the terrace of the next as it cascades down the sloping block, the complex is one of the most important examples of Inter-War Functionalist (Moderne) style design in Australia. The stepped communal gardens cascading down a hillside is based on a housing scheme outside of Oberammergau in Germany.

WYLDEFEL GARDENS (1936)
8 Wylde St, Potts Point
Architect: John Brogan

43

Wyldefel Gardens' heritage listing describes it as *"an important example of a client-driven application of aesthetics drawing from European examples in Germany and Italy in combination with more traditional influences from Canada. It demonstrates the early use of bent glass. The Art Deco interiors feature functional kitchens with new formica and magnesite finishes"*.

It was also described as *"arguably the most modern and striking example of residential architecture in Australia. It is a thoroughly integrated concept, combining interior with exterior, building with terrain, yet ensuring privacy from adjoining buildings with the openness of 'democratic' and communal central gardens. It is as much an experiment in living as it was a town planning or architectural project; its social objectives formed part of the news commentary of the day."*

In 1937, a year after completing Wyldefel Gardens the Crowles went away for three years. They came back to find the Navy had decided to extend Garden Island and that their house would go. Land reclamation by the Government during the war in Potts Point adjacent to the Naval dockyard meant that the house had to be demolished or removed, so in 1941 Crowle had his whole house moved piece by piece, put on a barge and ferried from Potts Point to its current location at Kurraba Point on the North Shore where it still stands.

🔍 *On the other side of Wylde St is The Gateway which sits right on a ridge which then drops away to Cowper Wharf Rd opposite the Navy shipyard.*

THE GATEWAY utilised a unique method of construction called portal slab construction where each concrete slab was laid down and then jacked up using pillars which became the principal and only supports. The walls were then left free of all impediments and were infilled with glass. As a result, the 34 apartments enjoyed unrivalled 270-degree panoramic views with only one common wall, spacious living rooms and floor-to-ceiling glass.

THE GATEWAY (1960)
3 Wylde St, Potts Point
Architect: C Smith

24

➜ *Follow the road down some 150m around the corner below Bomera and Tarana into Cowper Wharf Rd to see a different view of The Gateway and the Brutalist Navy car park.*

Brutalist Garden Island (Naval) car park, Woolloomooloo (1980) designed by John Andrews International

🔍 *The Brutalist Navy car park can be seen running for some 200m along Cowper Wharf Rd and best seen from the far side of the road where the ships are berthed. On top is Embarkation Park which we will visit a little later (p145).*

🔍 *The Gateway building can be seen above it on the left.*

← *Walk back up Wylde St on the west side for 100m till you reach Denison on the corner of Grantham St.*

DENISON (1966)
15 Wylde St, Potts Point
Architect: Hugo Stossel

25

➔ *Continue up Wylde St till you reach the little park area on the corner of St Neot Ave. Adjacent to 17 Wylde St (the curved white building you saw earlier) are a bank of Art Deco apartments along St Neot Ave.*

🔎 *Look into the foyer of 17 Wylde St before heading down St Neot Ave.*

BELVEDERE (1937)   **44**
21 St Neot Ave, Potts Point

19 ST NEOT (c1937)   **45**
19 St Neot Ave, Potts Point

TRENT BRIDGE (1938)   **46**
17 St Neot Ave, Potts Point

THE LACHLAN (c1939)
9-11 St Neot Ave, Potts Point
Architect: Charles Christian
47

THE LACHLAN was built as a private hotel with 21 rooms.

The south side of St Neot Avenue contains 5 3-storey Art Deco blocks of flats. These were probably all built around the same time in the late 1930s and perhaps coordinated by the same architect *(similar to those in Challis Ave pp150-151)*.

PARK VIEW (c1939)
7 St Neot Ave, Potts Point
Architect: Charles Christian
48

🔎 *At the end of St Neot you will see Serendipity which looks quite different when you go down the stairs and look at it again from the lower level of St Neot Ave.*

➔ *Follow the road a little further at the lower level and then turn left into Victoria St.*

SERENDIPITY (c1973)
3-5 St Neot Ave, Potts Point
Architect: Ian McKay

26

➜ *A few metres into Victoria St and you will be outside Harry Seidler's Gemini.*

➜ *Before you turn left into McDonald Lane continue up Victoria St for a few metres.*

GEMINI (1969)
40 Victoria St, Potts Point
Architect: Harry Seidler & Associates

27

The left tower was built in 1962 as Victoria Apartments with the second tower built in 1969, the complex renamed **GEMINI**. The buildings are linked by an overhead bridge footway. Seidler had a design flair for small spaces most of these being 38 square-metre apartments. The sky blue external aluminium roller-shutters are a feature.

145

- On your right is Embarkation Park, sited on the roof of the Navy car park, with beautiful views of the city and a nice place for a break.
- At the end of the park area are the McElhone Steps down to Woolloomooloo (100 steps).

Embarkation Park on the roof of the Navy car park

McElhone Steps down to Woolloomooloo

🔍 *Opposite the park is an unusual bank of terra-cotta coloured Victorian terraces with blue/green wooden railings and terraces.*

← *When finished turn back to McDonald Lane.*

Elegant bank of Victorian Terraces in Victoria St

➜ *Go up McDonald lane next to Gemini and within a few metres you will see Habitat on your left.*

Designed as apartments by Rudder Littlemore, who designed the famous former curved Qantas building in the city, the 'Florida Motel' or 'Florida Motor Inn' had a chequered career in the late 1960s and 70s. When threatened by Sydney Council the owners stated *'There are now no wild swimming parties that used to run to all hours of the morning and we have asked several girls of doubtful profession to vacate the premises.'* The building was sold, upgraded for apartments and renamed **HABITAT** in the late 1990s.

HABITAT (1964)
1 MacDonald St, Potts Point
Architects: Rudder Littlemore

28

➡ *Turn left at the top of McDonald Lane with Habitat on your left you will see the back of Chimes on your right. Behind you is the peach brick rear of Gloucester Hall which we will see in Challis St in a few minutes (p151).*

🔍 *When you get to McDonald St you can go left and have another look at L-shaped Habitat.*

🔍 *Opposite are 4 McDonald St and Manchester.*

Rear view of Chimes Apartments

CHIMES (1964)
45 Macleay St, Potts Point   **19**
Architect: Hugo Stossel

149

- 🔍 Above 4 McDonald St you can see the white concave back of 17 Wylde St (p128). This forms the outlook for all the kitchens and bathrooms in the building.
- ➜ Head back up McDonald St to Macleay St and at the corner have another look at Jenner House, 4 Macleay St and the Macleay Regis on the opposite side.
- ➜ Walk up Macleay St past Chimes and the Yellow House to the corner of Challis Ave.

MANCHESTER (1938)
2 McDonald St, Potts Point
49

4 McDONALD ST (c1938)
4 McDonald St, Potts Point
Architect: W C Brown
50

✱ *The Macleay St/Challis St area is a major restaurant hub for PP/EB with some 9 top eateries in a 50m radius.*

➔ *Just past Bistro 916 and Fratelli Paradiso are a line of four modest Art Deco apartment blocks which are worth a quick look as you check out the eating options on the other side (Fei Jai, La Bomba and Sopra).*

ESQUIRE appears modest from the front but the Functionalist style verandahs on the left-hand side facing the city are worth a look. The building contains 12 studios and 6 one-bedroom apartments

ESQUIRE (1938)
10 Challis Ave, Potts Point
Architect: Charles Christian

51

Charles Bohringer, the architect for three of these four buildings is important for a number of movie theatres he designed in NSW, Victoria and New Zealand. Of special note is his 1936 revamp of the Enmore Theatre with its extraordinary lighting (see *Sydney Art Deco*).

10A CHALLIS AVE (c1939)
10A Challis Ave, Potts Point
Architect: Charles Bohringer

52

THE CLIFT (c1939)
10B Challis Ave, Potts Point
Architect: Charles Bohringer

53

GLOUCESTER HALL is the most substantial of the group with 24 apartments comprising 4 2-bedroom, 12 one-bedroom and 8 bedsitter apartments. The original balconies were not filled in.

GLOUCESTER HALL (c1939)
10C Challis Ave, Potts Point
Architect: Charles Bohringer

54

➜ *Walking up Macleay St on the west side you can see Twenty on the opposite side with its serrated windows (probably adapted from Sodersten's CML Building in the city).*

🔎 *Twenty is better seen in winter as in summer it is heavily obscured by foliage.*

TWENTY (1936)
20 Macleay St, Potts Point
Architect: William Tarrant Broome

55

William Tarrant Broome who designed **TWENTY** was not registered as an architect, but he was also responsible for the design of 4 Macleay St a little further down Macleay Street. He was also at the same time charged with stealing over £3,000 over three years from the property sales office where he worked, using false cheques.

The serrated or 'zigzag' windows which are a major feature of the facade of Twenty are very similar to those of Emil Sodersten's buildings such as the CML Building (1936) and the former Byrant House in Pitt Street (1940). The stepped brickwork at the base of the first floor windows is lit from below at night and forms an elegant framing of the entrance. The building is substantially intact.

Serrated windows with stepped brickwork at base. Modern windows seem to have more surround and less glass than original.

Night-time view showing entrance and elegant effect of upward lighting on brickwork.

➡ *Reaching Challis Ave cross over Rockwall Crescent to be outside Zinc Cafe (which is ideal for coffee, breakfast and lunch).*

➡ *A few metres down Rockwall Crescent on the left-hand side is the Colonial villa, Rockwall.*

Rockwall (1837) Architect: John Verge

ROCKWALL was built between 1831 and 1837 in the Colonial Regency style and designed by the architect John Verge. Rockwall was one of the first examples of Colonial villa architecture (and landscape design) in Sydney reflecting changing tastes in England during the 1820s. Repeated financial crises in the colony saw major subdivisions of the original grants and by the 1920s only a handful of the original 20 or so grand villas in Potts Point remained. Rockwall was used as a girls' school and private hotel before returning to private ownership in more recent years.

➜ *At the end of Rockwall Crescent, St Vincent's College for girls can be seen through the gates, which contains a mixture of 19th and 20th century buildings.*

Another view of St Vincent's College from Victoria St at the corner of Challis Ave

ST VINCENT'S COLLEGE (1973)
Rockwall Crescent, Potts Point
Architect: Clement Glancy Jnr

29

← *Walk back to the corner of Macleay St and opposite Rockwall Crescent is The Macleay Hotel*

→ *A little further up the street is 40 Macleay St.*

✱ *As you walk up Macleay St you are passing the high-rise Ikon on the right which is on the site of the Chevron Hotel which used to host stars such as Frank Sinatra in the 1950s.*

THE MACLEAY was originally designed as a private hotel of 10 floors containing some 120 bedrooms.

Today The Macleay hotel has 126 serviced apartments and caters for interstate business people and travellers.

THE MACLEAY (1967)
28 Macleay St, Potts Point
Architects: Kann, Finch & Partners

30

Built in 1961, **40 MACLEAY STREET** operated as the Sheraton Marquee Hotel, with its most memorable guests being The Beatles who stayed in June of 1964. The building which consists of 9 floors and 2 underground car park levels, was converted to strata title in 1997 and today comprises 65 residential apartments and three commercial premises. A typical floor in the building is configured of 5 one-bedroom and 3 studio apartments. As well, there are 2 penthouses on level 9.

40 MACLEAY STREET (1961)
40 Macleay St, Potts Point
Architects: Miller & Farley

31

🔍 **On the corner of Macleay St and Manning Rd is Werrington with Wychbury next door.**

WERRINGTON (1930) and **WYCHBURY** (1934) are sister buildings designed by Emil Sodersten with a contrast in style from the earlier Werrington's more classical Tudor Gothic lines to Wychbury's Art Deco. Both buildings stand on land which was part of the Tusculum estate. They are both 8 storeys and the roof terraces were once connected.

Werrington and Wychbury in the late 1930s

WERRINGTON (1930)
85 Macleay St, Potts Point
Architect: Emil Sodersten
56

➜ *Walk a little down Manning Rd to get a good look at the brickwork at the entrance and the top of Wychbury.*

WYCHBURY (1934)
5 Manning Rd, Potts Point
Architect: Emil Sodersten

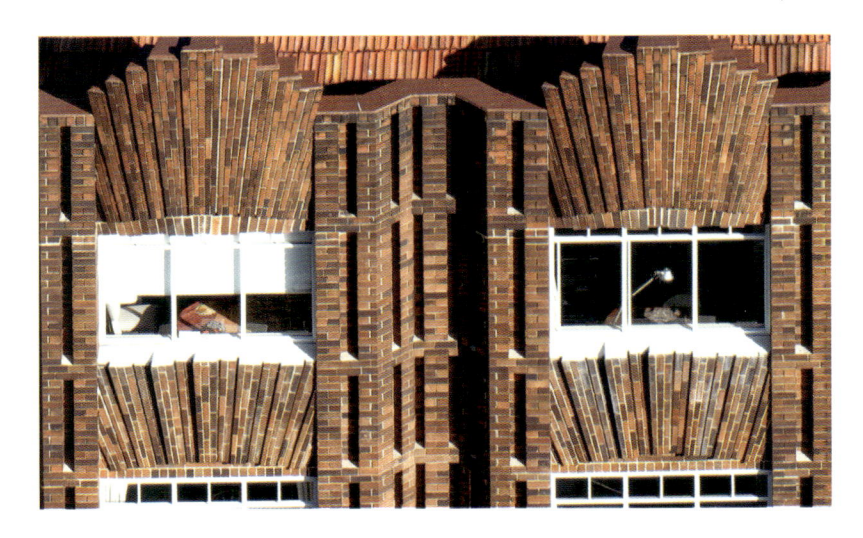

In **WYCHBURY**, built in 1934, the Art Deco influence is evident in the obvious vertical articulation and the geometric shapes of the brickwork. The four vertical bays are topped by fanned brickwork capping in the shape of sunbursts on the top two floors *(see above)*. This and the intricate stepped brickwork over the entrance shows Sodersten's mastery of the use of this material *(see below)*.

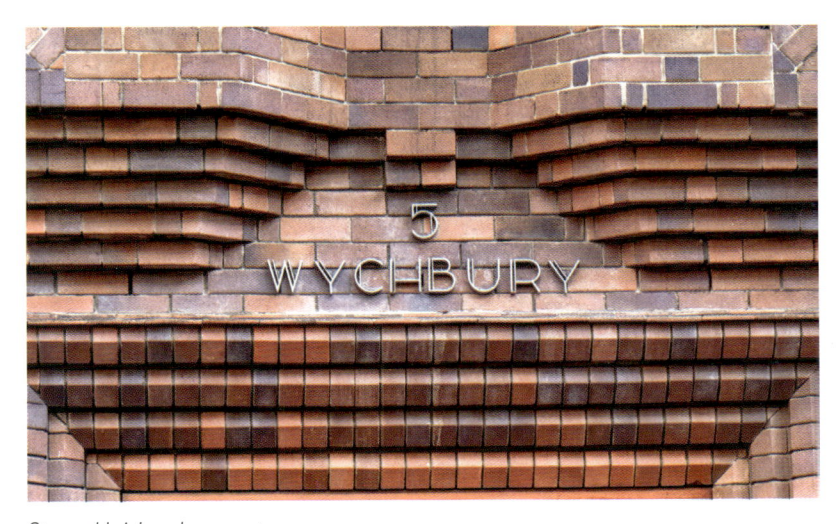

Stepped brickwork over entrance

➡ *Just past Wychbury is Tusculum from 1837.*
⬅ *Go back to the corner and over the road on the other side of Macleay St is Crick Ave with pale-coloured Devere Hotel on the corner and then Carlysle and West End in red brick further down the short dead-end street.*

TUSCULUM was designed by John Verge in Colonial Regency style and built between 1831 and 1837. Following its use as a serviceman's club during World War 2 and a private nursing home, the building fell into disrepair. Currently it is home to the Royal Australian Institute of Architects.

DEVERE HOTEL (1939)
44 Macleay St, Potts Point
Architect: Eric Pitt
58

This 5 storey block of residential flats had 35 bed-sits and 10 one-bedroom apartments. There were three shops facing Macleay Street and a kitchen and dining room on the roof.

CARLYSLE (1938)
2 Crick Ave, Potts Point
Architect: Rex Shaw
59

WEST END (c1938)
3 Crick Ave, Potts Point
Architect: R Pollock
60

← *To the left of the Devere Hotel is Manar which is an important local building.*

→ *Walk up to the lights and the crossing opposite Greenknowe Ave and look across at Kingsclere. Byron Hall is on your side of the road on the next corner.*

MANAR consists of a number of low-rise apartment blocks the first in 1919 emanating from an 1888 villa. Another two buildings at the rear and northern side, added between 1928-1938, are typical of the Inter-War architectural vibrancy prevalent in Potts Point during that time. Designed by Scott and Green in the neo-Georgian style with Palladian-proportioned windows, terrazzo foyers, Tuscan columns, ornate ceiling cornices with some modern Art Deco touches.

KINGSCLERE (1912) was the first high rise apartment block in the area and one of Australia's first block of flats. This prestige block in the Federation Free Style had 17 luxury apartments over 8 floors

BYRON HALL (1928)
97-99 Macleay St, Potts Point
Architect: Claud Hamilton

61

BYRON HALL (1928) designed by Claud Hamilton is variously described as Beaux Arts/Neo Gothic/Chicagoesque/Inter-War Classical Free Style perhaps with a few Art Deco touches. This and Franconia (p178) are the local examples of a transitional architectural style which by 1929 had shed the classical touches and become clearly Art Deco. Until the 1950s Byron Hall was serviced self-contained flats. Maids lived on the top floor and a caretaker resided on the ground floor.

- 🔍 *Looking further down Greenknowe Ave past Kingsclere is the imposing Tara and then 7 Greenknowe, a much smaller Art Deco building.*
- ➜ *You can cross over at the lights for a closer look and as you walk down Greenknowe Ave you can see the tops of Birtley Towers (p51) and Adereham Hall (p68) both seen earlier, dominating the skyline.*

TARA is an imposing 8-storey brick building sited on a corner block, just down Greenknowe Ave from the historic Kingsclere Apartments and showing the changes in architecture from 1912 to 1940. Its Art Deco brick exterior has two mirror image sides on both street fronts joined in a bevelled fashion with a single vertical mass of windows leading up to a castellated roofline. Originally named 'Texas' with some 160 apartments (144 bed-sitter and 16 one-bedroom) it was not completely finished till 1947, being interrupted during the war years and afterwards through national regulations and scarcity of labour and materials.

TARA (1941-1947)
3 Greenknowe Ave, Elizabeth Bay
Architect: D E Walsh

62

167

Tara is one of the few buildings in the area commenced during the war years. The entrance is in the laneway and has a Tudorish arch above the main entry. The foyer is in remarkably original condition with cream and black tiles and a tiled floor.

➜ **End up outside Byron Hall on the corner of Macleay St and Hughes St**

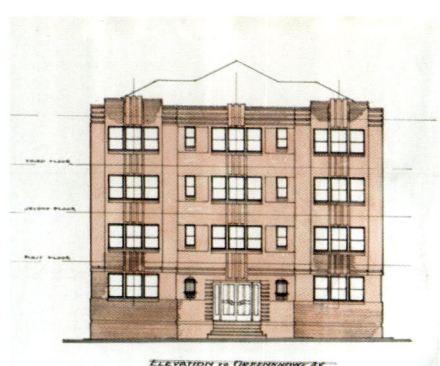

7 GREENKNOWE AVE

was completed well before its larger and more imposing neighbour Tara and originally contained 37 bed-sitter apartments.

7 GREENKNOWE AVE (c1939)
7 Greenknowe Ave, Elizabeth Bay
Architect: W T Broome

63

→ *Walk 50m down Hughes St to 25 Hughes St which shows some classical elements played out in the brickwork.*

25 HUGHES STREET has a simple brick Art Deco facade with vertical elements. The central section has some romanesque decorative features with the roof exhibiting a castellated parapet. The building contains 17 apartments, mainly one bedroom and studios. There is a rooftop terrace with city views.

25 HUGHES STREET (1931)
25 Hughes St, Potts Point
Architect: F Gordon Craig

64

➜ *Keep walking down Hughes St for another 20m and to your right on the corner of Tusculum Ave you will see the grand profile of Kanimbla Hall. The sunburst grills on the ground floor windows are probably original. Have a look through the two entrance doors at the simple wood-panelled foyers.*

KANIMBLA HALL (1938)
19 Tusculum Ave, Potts Point
Architect: G W Phillips

65

KANIMBLA HALL was originally 106 apartments in two sections with separate entrances. Some 16 were 2-bedroom apartments and the remainder (90) were one-bedroom.

The building is U shaped with a 5m wide courtyard in between the wings. The building has always been Company Title. The communal roof area has expansive views over the city and harbour.

← *Walk back to Macleay St, turn right and continue up 50m to the corner of Orwell St where you can see the red brick Gowrie Gate. Walk down Orwell St and check out the Gowrie Gate shops extending to the corner of Llankelly Place.*

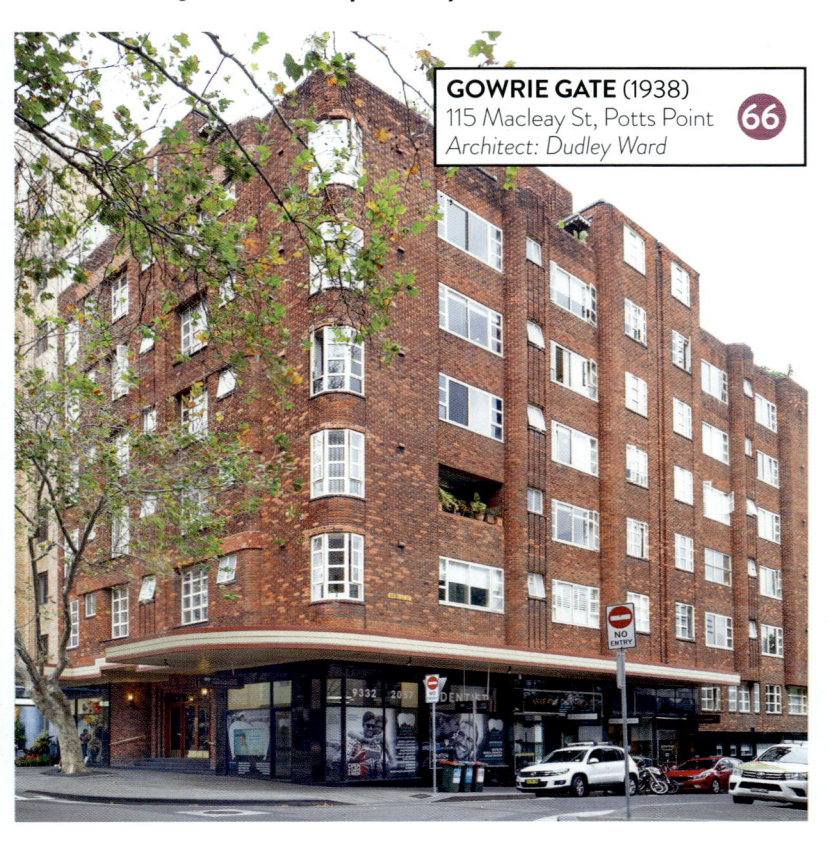

GOWRIE GATE (1938)
115 Macleay St, Potts Point
Architect: Dudley Ward
66

Dudley Ward's design for **GOWRIE GATE** and The Wroxton (p60) was informed by European architecture, particularly public housing in Germany and Holland. The building consists of 7 floors and a basement with the construction in red textured brick in the Art Deco style. When completed the building consisted of 53 self-contained flats, 4 penthouses, 2 professional suites and 6 shops facing Macleay Street and Orwell Streets. It is not clear whether the shops now facing Llankelly Place were part of the original design.

The shops were faced with black polished tiles and had curved windows at each entrance. The building originally featured a number of open balconies on the Orwell Street facade, but many of these have been infilled over the years to provide more living space.

View of rear of Gowrie Gate and Llankelly Place from Orwell St

Original shops along Orwell St side of Gowrie Gate *Trove, Decoration & Glass, Oct 1938*

🔍 *Where Gowrie Gate abuts Llankelly Place you can see the extraordinary Metro/Minerva theatre and the remainder of the original 3 building complex extending back to Macleay St.*

➡ *Walk down Orwell St a little further to see the elegant ziggurat shaped secondary building.*

METRO THEATRE (1939)
30 Orwell St, Potts Point
Architects: Bruce Dellit/Crick & Furse

67

The Metro/Minerva Theatre has had a long association with the nightlife of Kings Cross and Sydney's stage and screen world. It was designed by Bruce Dellit (who also designed the Anzac War Memorial in Hyde Park) and a more modest version was completed in 1939 by architects Crick and Furse after Dellit's death. An important Art Deco icon, The Metro/Minerva theatre is perhaps the best remaining commercial example in Australia of the Inter-War Functionalist style, which emerged in Australia in the 1930s, clearly influenced by American and European architecture of the time. Dellit's original designs were not fully realised including proposed sculptures by Rayner Hoff and a mural by Norman Lindsay. Nevertheless, the theatre's vertical and horizontal lines and curves symbolised the importance of progress and modernity and its relationship with the exciting medium of cinema. The main auditorium catered for 1000 people with luxury seating.

The interiors of the theatre were designed by Dudley Ward, the architect for Gowrie Gate (1938) directly opposite. The Metro was finally heritage listed in December 2020, hopefully forestalling damaging redevelopment and with the possibility for ultimate reinstatement as a live theatre venue.

🔍 *From the Gowrie Gate side of Orwell St you can see The Minerva Cafe & Nightclub which is today 'The Roosevelt Bar'.*

Original three building Minerva Complex 1939 Sam Hood (Collection of the State Library of NSW)

The theatre was part of a three building complex including the theatre and a cafe, nightclub and boutique shops extending from Macleay Street into Orwell Street. Next to the Minerva Theatre, the Minerva Cafe and Nightclub, built on the other side of Orwell Lane, featured a large semicircular pediment with vertical lines and a round, vaulted roof. The Minerva Building sat on the corner with Macleay Street with boutique shops such as a perfumery.

MGM converted the Minerva Theatre to a cinema in 1952 (renamed the Metro) in order to bring first-release films to Kings Cross and to reinvigorate the area as a *'new show centre'*. Australian promoter Harry M Miller returned live theatre to the Metro Kings Cross with the counterculture musical Hair, which opened on 5 June, 1969. The cast included Keith Glass, Reg Livermore and John Waters and the show ran to capacity audiences for two years, marking it as the longest and most successful of any Minerva/Metro show.

MINERVA CAFE & SHOPS (1939)
32 Orwell St, Potts Point
Architects: Bruce Dellit/Crick & Furse

68

* Llankelly Place is full of restaurants, bars and coffee shops.
➜ About 20m along Llankelly Place on the right is *Springfield Mall*. St James House is a modest but cute little narrow Art Deco building on the right-hand side.

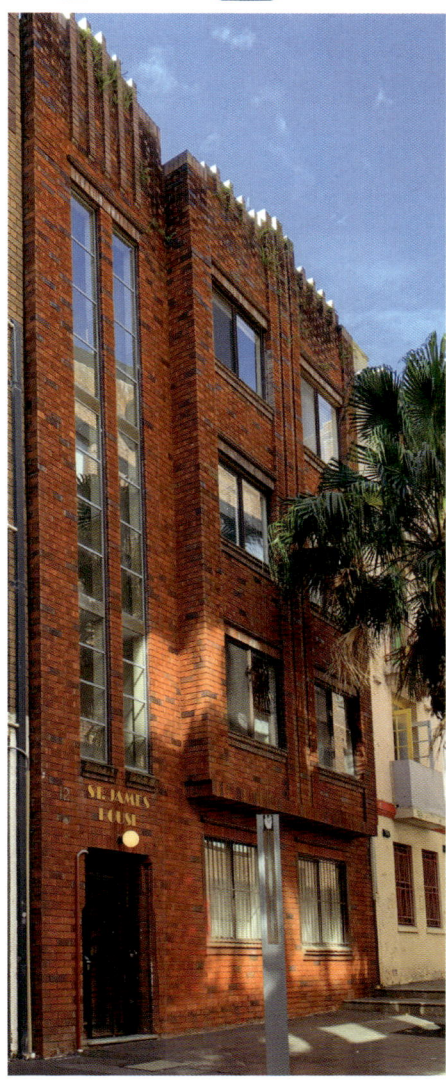

Front elevation from original plans

With 9 one-bedroom and 3 2-bedroom apartments **ST JAMES HOUSE** is actually in Springfield Mall although the address is Springfield Ave. The Art Deco typeface of the signage is quite special.

ST JAMES HOUSE (1936)
12a Springfield Ave, Potts Point

69

← *Go back to the corner of Macleay St and turn right.*

→ *Walk past the entrance to Gowrie Gate and look up to see the pressed metal Wunderlich ceiling and Art Deco features of the portico. Next door is Cahors with its blue tiles on the front.*

🔍 *Have a good look through the doors at the two level entry foyer.*

CAHORS (1941)
117 Macleay St, Potts Point
Architects: Joseland & Gilling

(70)

Two-level entry foyer

Cahors was built in 1941 on the site of the Cahors Villa. It is an iconic building in Potts Point and a fine example of a multi-storey Inter-War Art Deco style residential building with street level shops facing both Macleay Street at the front and Llankelly Place at the rear of the building. The building has pale buff face brickwork made by the Punchbowl Brick and Pipe Company. The base and canopy is in stark contrast to the colour of the brickwork, clad with striking pale blue terracotta tiles. Cahors' blue facade is actually the official colour of the French village of Cahors.

Cahors had 66 apartments and was very avant garde at the time with specially imported carpets, individually controlled refrigerators in the apartments controlled by a central compressor in the basement. The house telephone system was connected to the shops allowing orders to be immediately fulfilled. The entrance lobby, which contains fine original decorative features, is on two levels which adds to the gracious nature of the entry to the building.

In 1954 ASIO persuaded top-ranking Soviet agent Vladimir Petrov to hand over secrets about other KGB agents operating in Australia. They cultivated him with oysters, whisky and Kings Cross women. ASIO bugged him inside Cahors' third floor units. His wife was snatched back to Russia by the KGB but taken off the plane at Darwin in a dramatic diplomatic coup flashed around the world. They later lived in Sydney under pseudonyms.

→ *A few doors further up is Franconia. Across the road is our starting point and endpoint, the El Alamein Fountain, with Kingsley Hall in the background.*

FRANCONIA was completed at the end of 1929 in a Neo-Gothic style represented on the facade at street level with carved gargoyles, lanterns, coats of arms, stained glass doors, name font and various brass French fleurs-de-lis. It has some internal decorative elements in the Art Deco style. Furnished apartments were available for 4 pounds a week and included central heating, refrigerators, hot water and incinerators for household rubbish.

The name may reflect the ancient German-Frankish state of Franconia or may have been inspired by the visit of the Cunard Line luxury cruise ship, Franconia, which arrived in Sydney on a world trip in 1927, carrying 400 passengers.

FRANCONIA (c1928)
123 Macleay St, Potts Point
Architect: Walter Leslie Nielsen

71

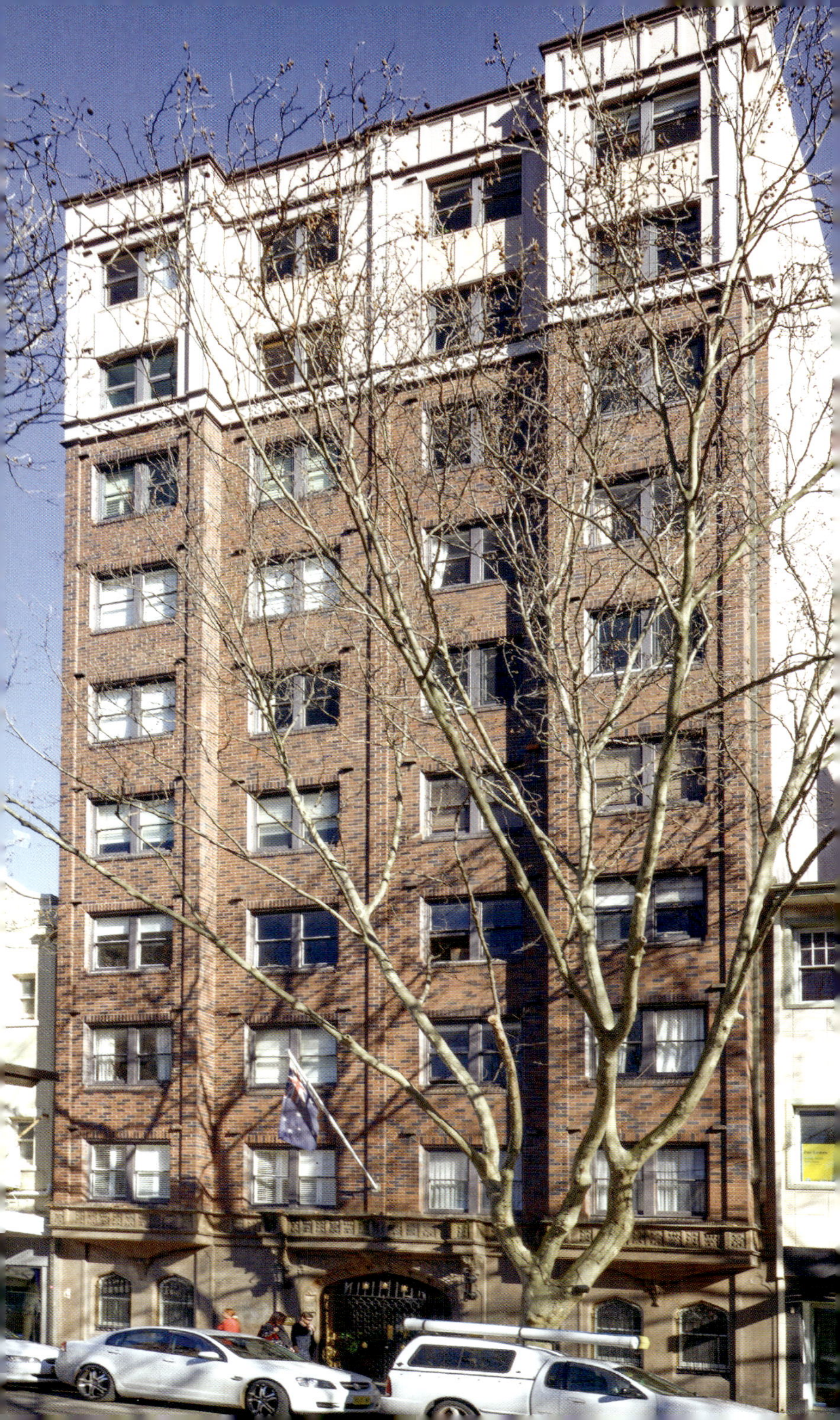

➤ *It is a 5 minute walk to see the Piccadilly Hotel which is not in great shape. Best route is walk back to Orwell St and follow it down to Victoria St (200m). Turn left and 70m along on the right is the Piccadilly Hotel.*

The heritage listed **PICCADILLY HOTEL** was constructed in 1939 for the Brewers, Tooths and Company, which replaced a previous hotel on the site called the Austral Club Hotel.

PICCADILLY HOTEL (1938)
171 Victoria St, Potts Point
Architects: Prevost & Ancher

72

It is a fine example of an Inter War Functionalist style building designed by prominent architects Prevost and Ancher. Unfortunately it has been in disrepair for some years awaiting redevelopment.

→ *Keep walking along Victoria St (south) and turn left into the tiny alley which is Earl Place. Follow this and you will pass Earl's Court and then next door the former Bernley Building and into Springfield Ave.*

BERNLEY BUILDING (c1938)
15 Springfield Ave, Potts Point
Architects: Crane & Scott

73

The former **BERNLEY BUILDING** was originally designed as a private hotel with some 25 rooms on each of the first 3 floors with communal showers and bathrooms on each floor. The fourth floor had 10 rooms leading on to the roof area which also contained a card room. The ground floor had a kitchen plus dining and lounge areas.

→ *Just along Springfield Ave on the right-hand side is Sandringham.*

← *Go back up through the open square to Darlinghurst Rd, with the Potts Point Hotel on your right. From here you can see the Bank Hotel* (2) *and Woolworths* (3) *a few metres to the right across Darlinghurst Road.*

→ *Turn left, go past the entrance to Llankelly Place and within a minute you are again in Macleay St opposite the El Alamein Fountain.*

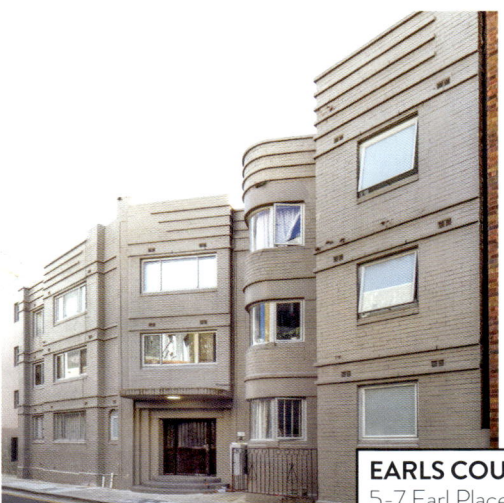

EARLS COURT is a 2-storey block with an original configuration of 30 one-bedroom apartments.

In the 5-storey **SANDRINGHAM** one can see Claud Hamilton's evolution to the Art Deco style from his earlier 1928 Byron Hall (p165)

EARLS COURT (1938)
5-7 Earl Place, Potts Point
Architect: Gordon McKinnon & Sons
74

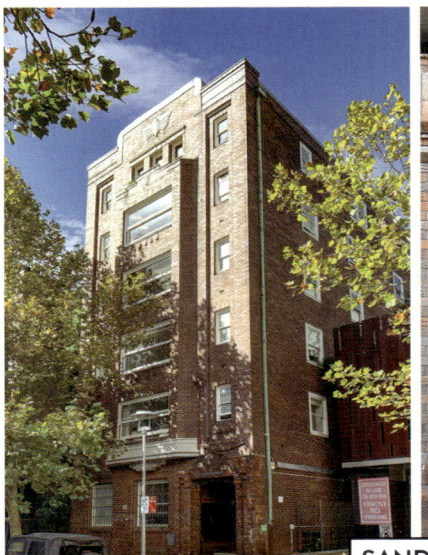

SANDRINGHAM (1935)
20-22 Springfield Ave, Potts Point
Architect: Claud Hamilton
75

* *Finally back where we started and behind the Modernist fountain both Art Deco and Modernist buildings are clearly seen (Gazebo & Kingsley Hall).*

The **EL ALAMEIN FOUNTAIN** was completed in 1961 as a memorial to the Australian Imperial Forces 9th Division and commemorates the Battle of El Alamein, Egypt, in World War 2. It is named for the Australian Infantry Forces (AIF) who fought near the Egyptian town of El Alamein in two battles which helped turn the course of the war.

EL ALAMEIN FOUNTAIN (1961)
Fitzroy Gardens Macleay St, Kings Cross
Architects: R Woodward & P Taranto

32

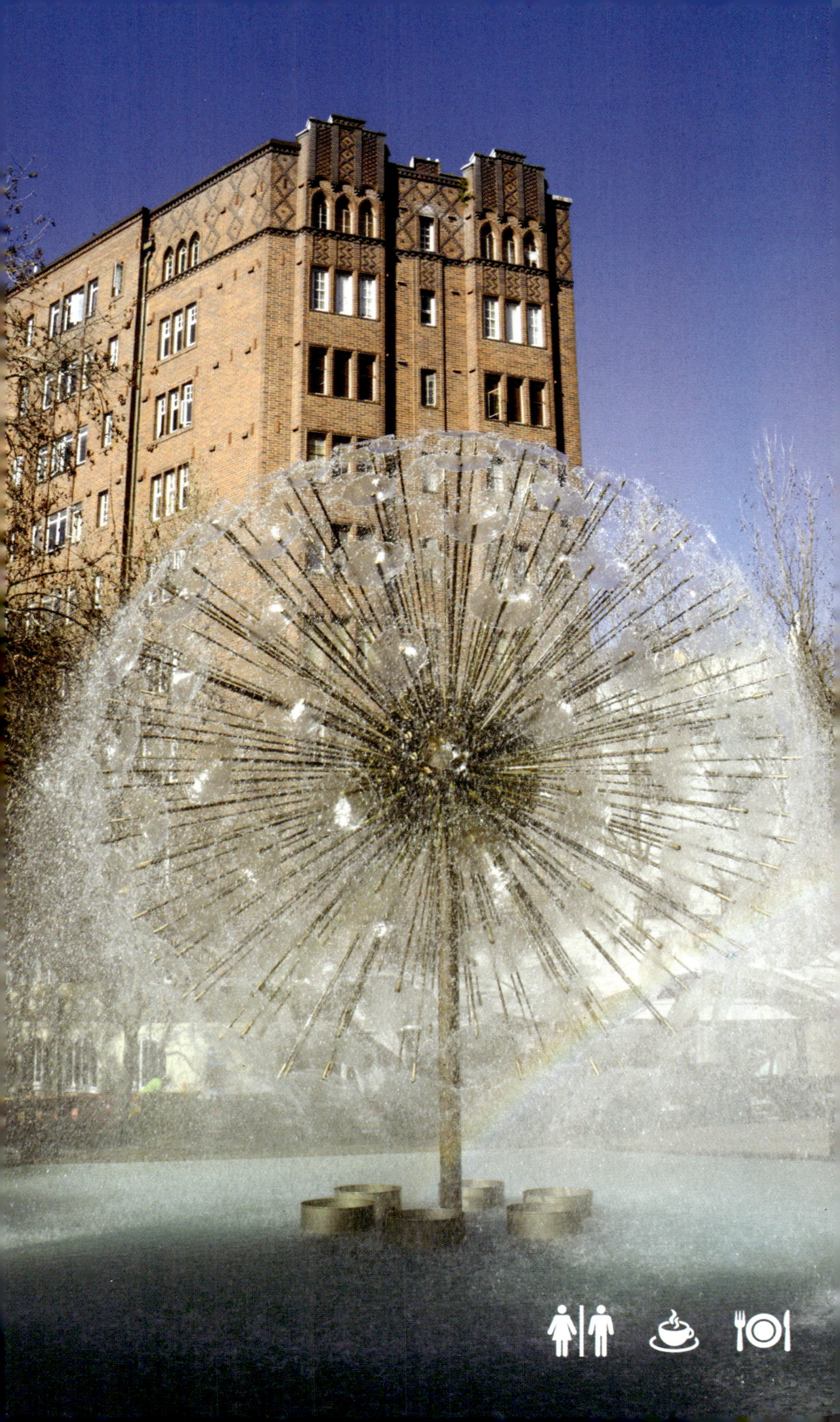

✱ On Saturday mornings the Kings Cross Organic Food Markets in Fitzroy Gardens have produce, flowers and food.

✱ *There are toilets near the Police Station to the left of Kingsley Hall*

✱ *Get a coffee at Café de la Fontaine (over the road at the lights) or a drink at Café Giorgio in front of Kingsley Hall.*
   YOU DESERVE IT !!

Kings Cross Organic Food Market - Saturday Morning in Fitzroy Gardens

WEST END
3
12
TWENT
ST. JAMES
HOUSE
FOUR
MACLEAY
STREET
DEL
THE VANDERBILT
WINST

DECO DOORWAYS

INDEX

INTER-WAR ART DECO

NAME	ADDRESS	MAP REF	PAGE
4 McDonald St	4 McDonald St PP	50	149
5 Onslow Ave	5 Onslow Ave EB	34	111
7 Greenknowe Ave	7 Greenknowe Ave PP	63	168
10a Challis Ave	10a Challis Ave PP	58	150
17 Wylde St	17 Wylde St PP	41	126
19 St Neot	19 St Neot Ave PP	45	141
21b Billyard Ave	21b Billyard Ave EB	29	100
25 Hughes St	25 Hughes St PP	64	169
76 Elizabeth Bay Rd	76 Elizabeth Bay Rd EB	15	57
Adereham Hall	71 Elizabeth Bay Rd EB	17	68
Ashdown	96 Elizabeth Bay Rd EB	19	78
Bank Hotel (fmr)	42 Darlinghurst Rd KX	2	36
Bellevue Gardens	20 Wylde St PP	42	130
Belvedere	21 St Neot Ave PP	44	141
Bernley Building	15 Springfield Ave	73	184
Billyard Gardens	8 Billyard Ave EB	32	104
Birtley Towers	8 Birtley Place PP	12	51
Boomerang	42 Billyard Ave EB	25	94
Byron Hall	97-99 Macleay St PP	61	165
Cahors	117 Macleay St PP	70	178
Carlysle	2 Crick Ave PP	59	163
Caversham Court	25 Billyard Ave EB	26	96
Chatsbury	6 Ithaca Rd EB	21	82
Del Rio	22 Billyard Ave EB	31	102
Devere Hotel	44 Macleay St PP	58	162
Earls Court	5-7 Earl Place PP	74	185
Edgewater	6 Billyard Ave EB	33	106
Eltham	18 Onslow Ave EB	14	56
Esquire	10 Challis Ave PP	51	150
Eurambie Hall	94 Elizabeth Bay Rd EB	20	80
Four Macleay St	4 Macleay St PP	40	124
Franconia	123 Macleay St PP	71	180
Gloucester Hall	10c Challis Ave PP	54	151
Gowrie Gate	115 Macleay St PP	66	172
Harley	1 Birtley Place PP	10	48
Huntingdon	8 Onslow Ave EB	36	113
Ithaca	4 Ithaca Rd EB	22	84
Kanimbla Hall	19 Tusculum Ave PP	65	170

INTER-WAR ART DECO (cont'd)

NAME	ADDRESS	MAP REF	PAGE
Kanimbla Hall	19 Tusculum Ave PP	65	170
Kingsley Hall	1a Barncleuth Sq PP	1	34
Macleay Regis	12 Macleay St PP	39	118
Manchester	2 McDonald ST PP	49	149
Marlborough Hall	4 Ward Ave PP	6	42
Melrose	23a Billyard Ave EB	27	98
Metro Theatre	30 Orwell St PP	67	174
Meudon	13 Onslow Ave EB	37	114
Minerva Café & Shops	32 Orwell St PP	68	176
Oxley	12 Ward Ave PP	5	40
Park View	7 St Neot Ave PP	48	142
Pembroke Hall	36B Macleay St EB	35	112
Piccadilly Hotel	171 Victoria St PP	72	182
Sandringham	20 Springfield Ave PP	75	185
Selsdon	16 Macleay St PP	38	117
Seventeen	17 Elizabeth Bay Rd EB	11	50
Somerset	23 Billyard Ave EB	28	99
St James House	12a Springfield Ave PP	69	177
Tain	21a Billyard Ave EB	30	100
Tara	3 Greenknowe Ave	62	166
The Clift	10b Challis Ave PP	53	151
The Harvard	2 Kellett Way PP	4	38
The Lachlan	9-11 St Neot Ave PP	47	142
The New Yorker	9 Ward Ave PP	7	44
The Roosevelt	3 Ward Ave PP	8	45
The Vanderbilt	2 Ward Ave, PP	9	45
Trent Bridge	17 St Neot Ave PP	46	141
Twenty	20 Macleay St PP	55	152
Ulverstone	65A Elizabeth Bay Rd EB	18	71
Werrington	85 Macleay St PP	56	158
West End	3 Crick Ave PP	60	163
Westchester	24-26 Onslow Ave EB	13	54
Winston	2a Ithaca Rd EB	23	86
Woolworths	50-52 Darlinghurst Rd KX	3	37
Wroxton	22 Roslyn Gardens EB	16	60
Wychbury	5 Manning Rd PP	57	160
Wyldefel Gardens	8 Wylde St PP	43	134

MODERNIST

NAME	ADDRESS	MAP REF	PAGE
20a Wylde St	20a Wylde St PP	20	129
40 Macleay St	40 Macleay St PP	31	157
76 Roslyn Gardens	76 Roslyn Gardens	7	65
Alexander Apts	4 Elizabeth Bay Rd EB	2	47
Aquarius	50 Roslyn Gardens EB	8	66
Ashleigh	104 Elizabeth Bay Rd EB	13	74,92
Bayview	41-49 Roslyn Gardens EB	5	63
Brentwood Gardens	90-92 Elizabeth bay Rd EB	15	81
Chimes	45 Macleay St PP	19	123,148
Denison	15 Wylde St PP	25	140
El Alamein Fountain	Fitzroy Gardens PP	32	186
Elizabeth Bay Gardens	15-19 Onslow Ave	17	115
Elizabeth Gardens	1 Holdsworth Ave EB	4	59
Ercildoune	85 Elizabeth Bay Rd EB	9	72
Fairhaven	8 Wylde ST PP	23	133
Gazebo	2 Elizabeth Bay Rd PP	1	46
Gemini	40 Victoria St PP	27	144
Gweedore	12 Wylde St	22	131
Habitat	1 MacDonald St PP	28	147
HMAS Kuttabul	18 Wylde ST PP	21	129
International Lodge	100 Elizabeth Bay Rd EB	14	76
Ithaca Gardens	12 Ithaca Rd EB	3	58
Karingal	5-7 The Esplanade EB	16	16
Murrawan Court	3 Elizabeth Bay Cr EB	10	73
Macleay Gardens	8 Macleay St EB	18	108
Oceana	108 Elizabeth Bay Rd EB	11	74,92
Riviera	106 Elizabeth Bay Rd EB	12	74,92
Serendipity	3-5 St Neot Ave PP	26	143
St Vincent's College	Rockwall Cr PP	29	155
The Gateway	3 Wylde St PP	24	136
The Macleay	28 Macleay St PP	30	156
Tor	51 Roslyn Gardens	6	64

SYDNEY ART DECO

Released 2019
Reprinted 2021
RRP $99

This is the first reference book on Sydney's Art Deco architecture with 800 full colour contemporary images and 200 b&w archival photos.

Containing 432 pages highlighting 350 commercial, civic and industrial buildings plus houses, apartment blocks, cinemas and shops. Important historical details are included along with condensed summaries. In excess of 100 local architects are identified.

Sydney Art Deco presents, as a counterpoint to the buildings, examples of artwork from some of Australia's best artists who lived and painted in Sydney at the time including Margaret Preston, Grace Cossington Smith, Roland Wakelin and Dorrit Black. Additionally, the photography of Sam Hood, Harold Cazneaux and Max Dupain is featured in the archival images, giving the reader a sense of yesterday next to today. A beautiful coffee-table book that can be enjoyed at every level.

Available from all good bookshops, online booksellers or peter@petersheridan.com

PAGE

19th CENTURY VILLAS

Ashton	75
Bomera	132
Edgerley	102
Elizabeth Bay House	109
Jenner House	125
Rockwall	154
Tresco	75
Tarana	132
Tusculum	162

POINTS OF INTEREST

Beare Park	90
Deco Doorways	190
Embarkation Park	145
Fitzroy Gardens	188
Kingsclere	164
Kings Cross Organic Food Market	188
Manar	164
McElhone Reserve	110
Navy Car Park	138
McElhone Stairs	145
Rushcutters Bay Park	59
Stairs from Billyard Ave to Macleay St	116
Victorian Terraces	62, 146
Yellow House	122

Join the
Art Deco & Modernism Society of Australia

**TALKS | EVENTS | WALKS
4 JOURNALS A YEAR
CALENDAR | CONGRESSES**

P.O. Box 17, Camberwell, VIC 3124
robingrow@ozemail.com.au
Tel: +61 3 6860978
artdeco.org.au

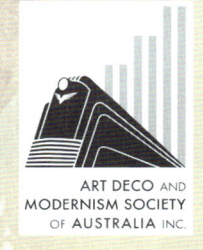

ART DECO AND
MODERNISM SOCIETY
OF AUSTRALIA INC.

NOTES

COMING SOON
IN 2022

SYDNEY
Art Deco & Modernist
CENTRAL BUSINESS DISTRICT
WALKS

Peter Sheridan

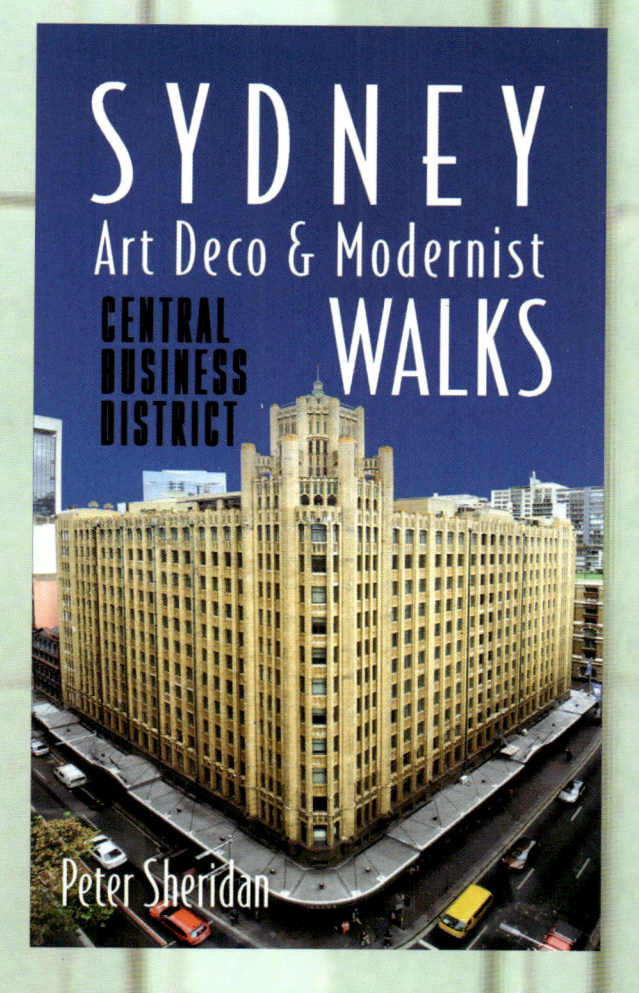

Companion to the Potts Point / Elizabeth Bay Walking book
Highlighting the city's 80 Art Deco, Modernist and Brutalist buildings
ll of photos, history, maps and an expert guide to the best of 20th century architecture in Sydney's CBD

order advance copies from peter@petersheridan.com

NOTES